Careers in Media and Communication

Stephanie A. Smith
Virginia Tech

Los Angeles | London | New Delhi
Singapore | Washington DC | Melbourne

FOR INFORMATION:

SAGE Publications, Inc.
2455 Teller Road
Thousand Oaks, California 91320
E-mail: order@sagepub.com

SAGE Publications Ltd.
1 Oliver's Yard
55 City Road
London, EC1Y 1SP
United Kingdom

SAGE Publications India Pvt. Ltd.
B 1/I 1 Mohan Cooperative Industrial Area
Mathura Road, New Delhi 110 044
India

SAGE Publications Asia-Pacific Pte. Ltd.
3 Church Street
#10-04 Samsung Hub
Singapore 049483

Printed in Canada

Library of Congress Cataloging-in-Publication Data

Names: Smith, Stephanie, 1985- author.

Title: Careers in media and communication / Stephanie Smith, Virginia Tech.

Description: Thousand Oaks, California: SAGE, [2019] | Includes bibliographical references and index.

Identifiers: LCCN 2017052260 | ISBN 9781506360928 (pbk. : alk. paper)

Subjects: LCSH: Mass media—Vocational guidance. | Communication—Vocational guidance.

Classification: LCC P91.6 .S65 2019 | DDC 302.23/023—dc23 LC record available at https://lccn.loc.gov/2017052260

This book is printed on acid-free paper.

Acquisitions Editor: Terri Accomazzo
Editorial Assistant: Sarah Wilson
Production Editor: Laureen Gleason
Copy Editor: Megan Markanich
Typesetter: Hurix Digital
Proofreader: Victoria Reed-Castro
Indexer: Mary Mortensen
Cover Designer: Dally Verghese
Marketing Manager: Jenna Retana

19 20 21 22 10 9 8 7 6 5 4 3

Careers in Media and Communication

Sara Miller McCune founded SAGE Publishing in 1965 to support the dissemination of usable knowledge and educate a global community. SAGE publishes more than 1000 journals and over 800 new books each year, spanning a wide range of subject areas. Our growing selection of library products includes archives, data, case studies and video. SAGE remains majority owned by our founder and after her lifetime will become owned by a charitable trust that secures the company's continued independence.

Los Angeles | London | New Delhi | Singapore | Washington DC | Melbourne

BRIEF CONTENTS

DETAILED CONTENTS

MASS COMMUNICATION

Upon opening this book, I'm going to assume you are either beginning to think about your college major and potential career or beginning to think about your postgraduate career. Understanding the concepts and how industries you have spent years learning about conduct business is essential in choosing the best fit for you. You have likely encountered some course or lesson on mass communication, or perhaps you spent your entire collegiate career studying the field. However, since multiple definitions exist, it is worth discussing the most accepted and dominant view as well as briefly reviewing the history of the field and popular theories of mass communication. Then we can begin to discuss relevant skills and career opportunities.

WHAT IS MASS COMMUNICATION?

There are three scholars who each define *mass communication* slightly differently. DeFleur and Dennis (1993) define it as "a process in which professional communicators use media to disseminate messages widely, rapidly and continuously to arouse intended meanings in large and diverse audiences in attempts to influence them in a variety of ways." Orlik (1992) says, "Mass communication is the process of rapidly conveying identical information, assertions and attitudes to potentially large, dispersed and diversified audiences via mechanisms capable of achieving that task." Finally, Berger (1995) argues that mass communication "involves the use of print and electronic media such as newspapers, magazines, film, radio or TV to communicate to the large number of people who are located in various places often scattered all over the country or world."

What do these three definitions have in common? They all focus on message dissemination to a large audience, through various channels, to accomplish some type of goal. However, these definitions focus on how mass media is studied, not necessarily how it is practiced. Mass communication is the study of how people and entities relay information through the mass media. Mass *media* is the practice of using media technologies to reach a large audience through mass communication. Therefore, the two are interdependent upon one another.

Mass communication and mass media encompass a variety of industries including, but not limited to, publishing (newspapers, magazines, and books); radio, TV, and film; advertising; social media; and public relations (PR). Mass media also influence how business is conducted and how people communicate within public and private sectors and within nonprofit organizations (NPOs). A main differentiating factor between mass communication and other forms of communication (such as nonverbal or interpersonal) is that mass media focus on one source transmitting information to a large number of receivers. The main focus of study, then, is how that communication can influence the behavior of others, a key component for effective business operations.

THEORIES OF MASS COMMUNICATION

If you studied mass communication throughout college, these theories should not be foreign to you. If you have not encountered mass communication theory yet, that is okay. Theory does not disappear when you graduate. In fact, theory helps guide our practice of mass communications and engage with mass media strategically. Theory is also essential in understanding human behaviors and responses, a key in campaign planning and evaluation. A brief overview of four foundational and commonly used theories follows. Your understanding of these theories and how they relate to practicing mass communications will help you choose an industry that is the best fit.

Cultivation Theory

This is one of the most popular and widely used mass communication research theories. Cultivation theory argues that television viewing can change a person's perception of reality over time. For example, exposure to television has influenced how people learn about and practice traditional roles and behaviors within society, such as gender roles (Gerbner, 1998). Cultivation theory operates with three main assumptions, focusing on the medium, the audience, and thirdly, the functionality of the medium on the audience (Gerbner, 1998). In less abstract terms, television is a unique medium and shapes the way people think and relate to each other, but the effects are limited. Cultivation theory has primarily been studied with regard to violence on television but has also been used to examine music videos; lesbian, gay, bisexual, transgender, and queer (LGBTQ) issues; and children's health. An understanding of cultivation theory would be especially useful for pursuing a career in a television-related industry, such as production or advertising.

Uses and Gratifications Theory

Uses and gratifications theory is a relatively simple theory that can be useful for those working mass communication industries. The theory examines why and how people seek out specific media to satisfy specific needs (Ruggiero, 2000). For example, if someone wanted to know about an upcoming public event, where would they look for that information and why? This theory is unique because it takes an audience-centered approach to understanding mass communication. The theory implies that media compete with each other for the attention of the viewer. Therefore, mass communication professionals need to understand how to best position themselves within the media marketplace in order to reach their target audiences. Uses and gratifications research has provided insight into the different reasons why people use their mobile phones, the Internet, social media websites, online gaming platforms, and entertainment media.

Agenda Setting Theory

Although media cannot tell us what to think, they can tell us what to think about. This is called agenda setting. Agenda setting theory has two main assumptions: The first assumption is that the press and the media do not reflect reality; they filter and shape it. The second assumption is that media concentration on a few issues leads the public to perceive those issues as more important than others (McCombs & Shaw, 1972). While this theory was originally applied to political contexts, it has been applied to a variety of industries including business, advertising, and crime as well as interpersonal and international communication.

Two-Step Flow Theory

The two-step flow theory argues that most people form their opinions from opinion leaders who are influenced by mass media. It is two steps because the information flows from media to opinion leaders and then from opinion leaders to a broader audience (Katz & Lazarsfeld, 1955). Opinion leaders are often seen as more trustworthy and less biased than media sources. Therefore, they can have greater influence on large groups of people. In today's society, opinion leaders can be found on national news outlets, in publications, and used by businesses to promote and advertise products online. Bloggers have become especially influential opinion leaders and demonstrate the practicality and prevalence of the two-step flow theory in business practices.

MASS COMMUNICATION METHODS

As a professional in mass communication, you will undoubtedly undertake the execution and evaluation of a communication campaign. Understanding the most relevant and commonly used methods will give you a head start in the workplace. Additionally, being able to show value to senior management requires data and evaluation. The methods presented can help you plan and evaluate mass communication efforts in various industries. The first two methods are quantitative, while the last two are qualitative research methods.

Survey

Survey research, in broad terms, aims to generate data used to make generalizations about large groups of people. Within the field of mass communication, surveys can be helpful for copy testing, evaluating products or campaigns, customer service, and environmental scanning. Surveys can also be helpful in gathering demographic data on specific groups for more targeted communication tactics. Organizations can conduct surveys online, over the phone, through the mail, or even in person, like market research for instance. Surveys are valuable because they can help assess thoughts, opinions, and feelings from a desired audience, making pre- and posttesting of campaigns or products through surveys a commonly used method. Surveys can contain open- or closed-ended answer choices, but surveyors should be aware of respondent bias while answering. Oftentimes, respondents will select the more appropriate answer, regardless of whether or not that answer is honest. Although surveys are a fast and cost-effective method for organizations, the pros and cons of survey research should be weighed before implementation.

Content Analysis

Content analysis, sometimes called textual analysis, is the process of identifying categories from a specific type of communication to see what the content of that communication typically includes. There are five different sources of text that can be used in content analysis: (1) written; (2) oral; (3) iconic (drawings, paintings, icons); (4) audiovisual (AV; television programs, movies); and (5) hypertexts, which are online texts. Content analysis is a popular method in mass communication to understand "who says what, to whom, why, to what extent and with what effect?" (Lasswell, 1942). This can help identify a media slant or bias about particular issues and showcase trends that will influence future communications. Content analysis is especially popular in PR to help measure the success of a campaign. This method can demonstrate the frequency, length, and valence (positive or negative) of communication, which is valuable information for clients.

Focus Groups

This form of qualitative research brings a group of people together to discuss their thoughts and opinions toward something. For instance, an advertising company could hold a focus group to determine which advertisement is more effective and why, using the opinions expressed from the group. The interactive nature of focus groups sets them apart from other research methods. A discussion guide is created in advance to facilitate organized conversation among the participants and maintain the integrity of the method. The researcher or group moderator should take careful notes and/or record the audio of the focus group for later playback and evaluation. Focus groups are used heavily within marketing during the product development stages to help determine the direction of marketing initiatives. Focus groups are typically less expensive than other forms of market research but can be time consuming. Participants must be chosen carefully based on demographics, psychographics, attitudes, and behaviors (Lindlof & Taylor, 2011).

Observation

Often used as a preliminary method to help gather a starting point for additional research, observation is a systematic data collection approach whereby researchers engage their senses to examine people in natural settings (Lindlof & Taylor, 2011). Observation is best utilized for answering "how" or "what" type of questions when the topic is relatively unexplored and when it is important to understand a phenomenon in a natural setting. For example, think back to when the iPhone first came out. This revolutionized the way people engaged with their mobile phones. Observation helps us understand that people can no longer stand in elevators, ride in cabs, or even check in for flights without using their mobile phones. Although participant observation is the most commonly practiced form, observation can also occur using video or audio recordings. It is imperative that any person conducting observation research takes field notes that record their thoughts and preliminary analysis. Observation is an essential part of understanding naturalistic settings and can provide the foundation for theory and hypothesis development (Lindlof & Taylor, 2011).

MASS COMMUNICATION IN SOCIETY

Mass communication plays four main roles within society: surveillance, interpretation, socialization, and entertainment. Surveillance refers to how mass communication relays news and information to the public and, in today's society, how we also use media to monitor people and issues. This function of mass communication is important in establishing a connection between organizations and people (Bradley, 2016). People feel connected and informed by using online communication tools. For example, in times of natural disasters, war, or health scares, the media create awareness and keep us updated through surveillance of the situation.

Interpretation refers to how people form and express their opinions (Lasswell, 1948). The mass media set a context for new information and provide commentary about the significance and meaning of issues. Agenda setting is a theory used to help explain this function of mass communication. The media's selection of news and portrayal of issues affects how society understands and responds. For example, the media's reporting can often change the mind-sets of society depending on how and what they report.

Mass communication helps people learn socialization and cultural norms. Mass media transmits values within a society that help people learn appropriate behavior and attitudes. Television programs tend to reflect the societal norms of the area in which they are broadcast. This helps promote cultural understanding and socialization. Children's programming is a great example of this. Shows such as *Sesame Street* showcase good behavior and help instill moral standards in children who watch the show.

Finally, mass communication is a form of entertainment. We often turn to media outlets when we want to relax or escape everyday life. Mass media can also help us experience things that we would not otherwise be able to, like sporting events or award shows. We can use mass media to play games, communicate with others, form and maintain relationships, and relieve stress. Uses and gratifications theory research is especially helpful in understanding how people use mass media for entertainment.

TRENDS IN MASS COMMUNICATION

Technology has changed how we transmit, interpret, and receive information. Within the field of mass communication, technology is the driving force behind the three biggest trends: (1) social media, (2) digital news, and (3) mobile communication. We use technology for all four of the functions previously discussed—and so do organizations. In a society where a constant connection is expected and valued, technology has changed how we communicate and, thus, changed how information is shared with publics.

Currently, there are roughly three billion Internet users and over two million social media users (Smith, 2016). It then stands to reason that 91% of retail brands actively use social media channels to communicate with their stakeholders (Kemp, 2016). Given the way that social media has infiltrated our lives, mass communication organizations such as those that will be discussed in this book are forced to integrate social media into their business plans. In fact, 80% of businesses now have a dedicated social media team (Holmes, 2015). Social media is not going anywhere, so an understanding of how to leverage social media for business communications is required. Some businesses are now using their employees as online ambassadors (Holmes, 2015), and advertising on social media sites continues to rise in effort and impact year after year (Holmes, 2015). Social media has also helped everyday people become activists and helped notable faces communicate without gatekeepers and fabricated agendas, a blessing and a curse for PR practitioners. Finally, social media is revolutionizing how information is shared through mediums like video. Some companies even report video as their most effective marketing tool (Holmes, 2015). Considering how you personally use social media to share and receive information is important and is blurring the lines for how businesses share and receive information.

Advances and adoption of social media channels have changed how people consume news. Digital news is now more popular with most audiences than traditional news. Since the majority of U.S. adults now get their news online, publishers are forced to enter this realm and find creative ways to share news online (Gottfried & Shearer, 2016). While television still reigns supreme for news consumption, digital news sources are a close second place (Lu & Holcomb, 2016). Especially with regard to political news like elections, digital news sources are preferred by most people (Lu & Holcomb, 2016). Newspapers, radio programs, and television programs now integrate social media tactics into their programming through encouraging their audiences to tweet with them or follow them on Facebook to help boost their audience and online engagement. Podcasts and e-mail newsletters are two new takes on traditional media where publishers have taken proven communication techniques and updated them for the digital world. A majority of news websites offer online newsletters since a newsletter is a better way for the reader to digest the content. Similarly, podcasts can help better capture specific audiences to share information (Lu & Holcomb, 2016).

Smartphones, much like social media, have also changed our lives and our communication. Mobile communication no longer refers to calling someone and chatting. It now encompasses texting, sending high-resolution photos and videos, using FaceTime, social networking, gaming, and conducting business. Our phones essentially act as small computers, and we expect compatibility across platforms. Mobile communication presents an interesting opportunity and challenge for organizations. For example, among the 50 highest circulating daily newspapers, more than half of their traffic comes from mobile phone users (Lu & Holcomb, 2016). Businesses now have to ensure that their websites and content are mobile user-friendly, and some businesses have created specialized and customizable apps to further engage their mobile audience. In the next couple of years, be on the lookout for increased mobile communication platforms and further integration between organizations and their mobile audiences.

SKILLS

Although each industry and job requires a unique skill set, there are some basic skills that cut across industries and bode well for success in any field of mass communication. For example, being able to articulate your thoughts and the thoughts of others to a variety of different audiences, using multiple channels, is essential regardless of whether you work in news or nonprofits. Within each industry chapter, specific skills will be discussed. However, here are some of the absolutely necessary skills to acquire and sharpen for mass communication careers.

Analysis/evaluation
Business acumen
Cultural norms
Desire to learn
Editing
Human behavior
Production/design
Research
Writing

ADVERTISING AND MARKETING

How many times have you watched a television show like *Mad Men* or commercials and thought about how cool it would be to create advertisements or work for an advertising agency? If you're anything like me, the thought has crossed your mind more than once. Advertising is perceived as a fast-paced, glamorous industry, while marketing is often thought of as number crunching in a cubicle. In this chapter, you will learn about the fundamentals of both industries, how they work together, and the realities of working in advertising and marketing.

WHAT IS ADVERTISING?

In the simplest form, advertising is *paid* media. Advertising has also been defined as "an audio or visual form of marketing communication that employs an openly sponsored, non-personal message to promote or sell a product, service or idea" (Stanton, 1984, p. 465). Businesses are often the sponsors of advertising. The Advertising Educational Foundation (AEF; 2016) defines advertising as the *salesmanship* element that can make a difference between business success and failure. AEF (2016) further explains that the business of advertising involves marketing objectives and creative ability using both qualitative and quantitative research methods. The purpose of advertising is to persuade consumers that a company's services or products are the best. Advertising can also help enhance the image of a company, create needs for products, demonstrate new uses for existing products, and build brand loyalty. Advertising and marketing have an interdependent relationship and, thus, are often thought of in tandem. Further, advertisements are communicated through mass media including, but not limited to, radio, television, print, and social media.

Although the beginnings of advertising can be traced back to Egypt, China, and Europe in the 18th and 19th centuries, it was not until the 20th century that advertising exploded in the United States. Edward Bernays, often credited for his revolutionary work in public relations (PR), is also regarded as the modern founder of advertising (Wilcox, Cameron, & Reber, 2015). The Torches of Freedom campaign was an advertising and PR hybrid, but it is thought of as the first big advertising initiative in the United States. At the time, in 1920, it was taboo for women to smoke in public. Bernays, a heavy smoker himself, was hired by the American Tobacco Company to change the stereotype and encourage women to smoke in public. Bernays hired women to be photographed smoking in the New York Easter parade, and the Torches of Freedom movement was born. In the following years, the tobacco industry's advertising campaigns targeted at women increased sales to over 30% through a 30-year time span (O'Keefe & Pollay, 1996). Tobacco companies continued to advertise cigarettes to women as "torches of freedom" throughout the 1990s, thanks to Bernays.

Bernays' campaign changed the association of cigarettes and was revolutionary but also demonstrates how advertising is a channel for communicating cultural norms. Early advertising initiatives highlighted and encouraged a more modern lifestyle, of course relative to the time, and arguably helped many immigrants assimilate to an American way of life (Ewen, 2001). Moreover, advertising paved the way for women in business. Understanding that women were the primary decision makers and influencers within their families and personal social networks, advertisers capitalized upon their unique insight and engaged women during the brainstorming and creative phases of crafting campaigns (Ewen, 2001).

Advertising continued to evolve with advances in media. Radio programs were sponsored by businesses in exchange for a brief mention of their products. In the 1950s, advertisements appeared as television commercials. With the inclusion of cable television, specialty channels devoted to advertising emerged including QVC and the Home Shopping Network, now HSN. Then, the Internet created an opportunity for online, personalized, and interactive advertising.

Today, virtually any medium can be, and often is, used for advertising. The next time you're out doing something, take a few minutes to observe your environment, and count the number of advertisements you see. Billboards, websites, flyers, banners, text messages, e-mail, transportation vehicles, shopping carts, and even overhead speakers at gas stations provide opportunities for advertising. Did you notice that until you started consciously looking for advertisements, you didn't realize how many surrounded you? This is a challenge within the industry today because consumers are surrounded by so much "noise" and advertisers need to make their placements stand out. While the opportunities for advertising are seemingly endless, U.S. television advertising remains the leader, with revenue around $71 billion, just for 2015 (Statista, 2016). Digital advertising, however, is a close second and beats out the revenue generated by radio and newspaper advertising (Statista, 2016). It should come as no surprise given the revenue generated that the American advertising market today is the largest in the world, followed by China (Statista, 2016).

INSIDER INSIGHT

TIFFANY CHOI, ADVERTISING AGENCY ACCOUNT SUPERVISOR (PHARMACEUTICAL ADVERTISING)

What is your job description?

The role of an account supervisor is to be the day-to-day lead on client requests and projects. The individual develops trusting relationships with the client to help accomplish their strategic goals, ensures timelines are met with each deliverable, and facilitates the process of digital projects by working with the internal team (creative, strategy and/or analytics, project managers).

Describe a day in the life of your job.

On an average day, I do some or all of the following tasks:

- Manage monthly financials and invoicing
- Work closely with project managers to communicate timing of client projects
- Educate clients on the agency's expertise in digital programming and data collection processes
- Work closely with agency partners to help ensure goals and strategic imperatives are streamlined across resources
- Facilitate the asset handoff process between the internal team and agency partners for programming
- Review resources at each stage of submission in the medical, legal, and regulatory review process to help ensure all changes are captured correctly and the resource is free of errors

What are the biggest misconceptions about your industry?

A common misconception is that individuals working in account management work late nights all the time, have unrealistic deadlines, and overpromise deliverables to clients without the internal team's agreement. While yes, these may hold true at agencies from time to time, where I work, work–life balance is highly respected and the team pushes back appropriately when timelines are unreasonable.

What is the best professional advice you have received?

"No one is going to look out for you, besides you." This has inspired me to be confident as I transition to new agencies because I feel empowered to make changes in my career and explore other organizations.

(Continued)

(Continued)

How have mentors influenced your career?

Mentors have influenced my career a great deal. I had a mentor at Michigan State whom I met thought a career fair in 2008. Today, 8 years later, we are still in touch, and I've informed him of my career aspirations and my moves to different agencies. I've also kept in touch with my first boss from the first full-time agency I worked for. I've appreciated the honest, candid feedback I've received from them.

What are a few things you wish you had learned in school about your career?

There is no advertising class that can prepare you for working in an agency. At Michigan State, I studied advertising and took 4 years of classes that all involved group projects. The extent that others are able to do their job is something I learned then, and I had no idea how much it would still apply to my career now. My day to day is heavily dependent on how others do their job and the timeliness involved with doing so.

What do you love about working in your industry?

The people and the different personalities I come across working with various companies, projects, and skill levels.

What do you think are emerging trends within your industry?

The Affordable Care Act is an emerging trend. As cost and formulary coverage become more important for patients, it will be interesting to see how branded medications will be marketed to physicians—whether it is with value-add programs or incentives for patients or how efficacious a drug is versus a generic one.

With Fitbit and Apple watches trending, wearables are becoming more popular. The discussion around how accurate the tracking is and how patients are reporting these results to their physicians will become more of a topic in the doctor's office and, thereby, in my line of work.

What advice do you have for someone starting out in your industry?

- Don't be afraid to start at the bottom.
- It is okay to move agencies and find the best fit for yourself.
- Treat others the way you want to be treated.
- Never burn any bridges with old coworkers or managers. Advertising is a small world, and pharmaceutical advertising, like any niche, is even smaller. You never know who will be your next client or colleague.

What are the three most essential skills for success in your industry?

1. Be persistent. To be effective in account management, it is critical to overcommunicate with clients and the internal team. I find that follow-up is key, whether it is documenting a discussion or confirmation of next steps, or a recap after a meeting. No one should be guessing what the next steps are.
2. Be curious. Never assume you know the answer to something because there are always special exceptions to the rule. Ask questions!
3. Have a proactive attitude. I've learned to take initiative on many projects even if I'm unfamiliar with the content itself. When I have the opportunity to learn something new or try a new task that might be challenging, I try it anyway. I find that my effort is appreciated and respected by my colleagues.

How has networking influenced your professional life?

Networking has been an integral part of my career, particularly as I transition to new agencies. For example, I've found my last two jobs on LinkedIn. By simply responding to a recruiter's message, I've found opportunities that would be unknown if I was job searching using more traditional methods.

How do you suggest someone stay up to date on your industry and remain competitive?

- Read local and national news.
- Subscribe to relevant blogs.
- Be familiar with the work your agency or organization does and the accolades they have received.

MARKETING

What Is Marketing?

The American Marketing Association (n.d.) defines *marketing* as "the activity, set of institutions, and processes for creating, communicating, delivering, and exchanging offerings that have value for customers, clients, partners, and society at large." More simply, marketing is communication between an organization and the consumer with the goal of increasing the bottom line and maintaining relationships. The goal of marketing is to get the consumer to do something, which can include buying a product, supporting an issue, or providing feedback. Today, marketing is a consumer-oriented industry.

The American Marketing Association (n.d.) also defines *marketing research*, which is a secondary industry of marketing. Marketing research is "the function that links the consumer, customer, and public to the marketer through information used to identify and define marketing opportunities and problems; generate, refine, and evaluate marketing actions; monitor marketing performance; and improve understanding of marketing as a process. Marketing research specifies the information required to address these issues, designs the method for collecting information, manages and implements the data collection process, analyzes the results, and communicates the findings and their implications" (American Marketing Association, n.d.). Careers in marketing can be general or more specific to marketing research.

Marketing first began as production-based during the Industrial Revolution. Products were made only if producers knew they could sell them. Therefore, during this time, the focus was on producing and distributing products at the lowest cost possible (Adcock, Halborg, & Ross, 2001). As technology advanced and competition grew, marketing evolved into a more sales-oriented industry following World War II (Adcock et al., 2001). It was during this time that advertising and branding began to matter, and marketing efforts included the use of persuasion tactics (Adcock et al., 2001). The selling orientation continued through the 1950s but did not consider consumer wants or needs. Rather, during this time marketing focused on selling existing products and using sales and promotion techniques to achieve the highest sales possible.

Today, the role of marketing has morphed into relationship management between consumers and organizations. Although younger compared to other industries, marketing has proven to be an important component of business and society. Unlike advertising, marketing is a function of nearly every business, across all industries, including nonprofits. Within the for-profit sector, marketing helps bring in revenue. In nonprofit organizations (NPOs), marketing works to attract supporters who can make donations, fund-raise, and volunteer their time. Regardless of the type of organization or industry in which it operates, marketing is essential to success.

The role of marketing has also expanded beyond a seller orientation to help determine what consumers want and need and fill the gaps accordingly using marketing research. This is a more proactive approach. However, marketing today does receive criticism. For example, critics argue that marketing encourages people to purchase things they do not need. While this practice is not totally unheard of, it ultimately does not lead to longstanding and profitable relationships. Thus, it does not lead to long-term success (Ethics in Marketing, 2016). A second criticism is that marketers embellish products, also a criticism of advertising (Ethics in Marketing, 2016). In today's world, there are varying degrees of consumer protection, which help to eliminate exaggerations from any organization for fear of legal trouble. Moreover, using such tactics will not fulfill the ultimate goal of building long-term, loyal consumers.

Marketing efforts, much like advertising, cover a broad range of mediums; however, careers within marketing are often bifurcated between traditional marketing and digital marketing. Direct marketing is another avenue within marketing where organizations communicate with a predetermined audience such as existing consumers or people who live within a certain town (Adcock et al., 2001). Finally, branding is another area within marketing that offers career potential. Branding is the marketing practice of creating and/or maintaining a brand defined as "a name, term, symbol, or design, or combination of them which is intended to identify the goods and services of one seller or group of sellers and to differentiate them from those of competitors" (Kotler, 1991, p. 442).

Similarities and Differences of Marketing and Advertising

At this point, you're likely wondering why we are even talking about advertising and marketing within the same chapter. Well, these two fields have distinct similarities and differences despite their interdependency. The biggest thing to know is that advertising is a component of marketing. Advertising is a part of the overall marketing strategy, often referred to as a tactic, to help marketing reach goals (Duenas, 2010). Therefore, advertising is simply a part of marketing. Other parts of marketing, like briefly mentioned before, include research, design, analysis, sales, PR strategies, and so on.

Advertising initiatives are often very costly for a short-term impact. Therefore, advertising is not always the best fit for a marketing campaign, since marketing focuses on long-term impact. Sometimes earned media (PR) is more effective for marketing than advertising. Nonetheless, marketing is making the choice whether or not to use advertising tactics during campaign planning and implementation. Also, it is important to remember that the goal of advertising is to sell something. However, marketing often has larger goals that include sales but are not limited to sales, such as increasing consumer awareness and building brand loyalty. Marketing also focuses on the 4 Ps (product, price, promotion, place) while advertising is concerned only with promotion (Surbhi, 2015). Therefore, marketing has a broader scope than advertising. Lastly, marketing helps create the market for products and building a brand image, while advertising aims to grab the attention of the audience. In sum, advertising is marketing, but marketing is not advertising (Surbhi, 2015).

CAREERS IN ADVERTISING AND MARKETING

Advertising and marketing are popular industries for people to seek employment because of the vast opportunities and diversity of positions available. Most advertising and marketing jobs, and certainly entry-level jobs, require a bachelor's degree but do not require advanced education. Advertising and marketing jobs can be in-house with an organization where you essentially have one main client, the organization you work for. Or, you can work for an advertising or marketing agency where you have a variety of clients each with separate goals, budgets, and ideas. Typical entry-level advertising and marketing jobs have an annual salary range between $30,000 and $35,000 (Glassdoor, 2016). Here are some of the jobs available in advertising (AEF, 2016) and marketing (Monster, 2016):

New Business Coordinator or Manager

A coordinator role denotes entry-level work, while a manager position is one step above. As a new business coordinator or manager, you would help recruit clients through pitching your agency. This job would require identifying, qualifying, and reaching out to potential new clients (read: research-focused). You would also need to use strategic skills to identify problems for brands and brainstorm potential solutions through content outlines. This job is for agency work only. Beginning a career as a new business coordinator or manager can help you become a new business director, or a director of business development.

Account Executive

You can think of an account executive (often also referred to as an account coordinator or account manager, depending on level of experience) as the person who takes over the account from the new business manager. In this role, you serve as the main point of contact between your agency and your client. Typical tasks include coordinating processes, providing direction, responding to requests and inquiries, and building relationships and management. This job is widely available in advertising and marketing agencies. Account executive positions can lead to senior account executive positions, account director, or vice president of account services opportunities.

Copywriter

As a copywriter, you create a broad range of written concepts for various campaigns and mediums. You may be working on sales promotions, marketing initiatives, advertising campaigns, or promotional materials. This is a writing-intensive position available for in-house or agency-style work. This can lead to advancements such as creative director.

Producer

After the clients have been secured and the advertisements planned, they need to be produced. The producer role offers positions from entry to senior level and is responsible for producing the content requested. This can include preproduction,

production, and postproduction needs such as shooting, recording, and editing. Producers are needed in-house and within agencies.

Interactive Designer

The creative is essential in advertising and marketing. In this role, you will design concepts, advertisements, websites, and other content as needed. You seek to connect with consumers through designing high-quality, interactive content. There are entry-level and mid-level opportunities for designers. Some roles are specific to mobile design or online design, while other roles are generalist positions where you should be prepared to design for print and online mediums. A career in design can lead to becoming an art director or creative director.

Media Buyer or Planner

So, the client is secured, the copy and design is completed, and now the advertisement needs to be placed. That's where the media buyer or planner enters the equation. In this role, you will help purchase television, radio, print, or online media spots for advertising campaigns. This position will require research to determine the best outlets for media buying as well as financial aptitude to secure ideal buys based upon campaign initiatives. Media buyers or planners can move on to become senior media planners, media supervisors, or group media directors.

Strategic Planner

As a strategic planner, you will work across teams to help identify and deliver insights to uphold or improve brand reputation and communication solutions. This role requires an ability and willingness to conduct research, creative problem-solving solutions, and long-term planning capabilities as well as to have an understanding of different implementation strategies.

Brand Coordinator or Manager

Brand coordinators or managers work closely with strategic planners and the marketing team to ensure that the organization's brand and messaging is consistent throughout all communications. They help determine the brand, work with creative to establish logos and themes, create messaging, and help plan materials for distribution. This role also requires some analytical capabilities, strong communication skills, and the ability to work well in teams.

Analyst

Analysts are needed within advertising and marketing as well as for agency and in-house work. An analyst relies on market research to inform and inspire recommendations and should work well with all business areas and teams.

This job requires a strong attention to detail, analytical and math skills, and research skills. The analyst will help drive business insights by contextualizing data for all marketing channels.

Social Media Coordinator, Manager, or Specialist

A social media coordinator or manager helps to ensure consistent brand messaging and awareness across social media platforms. They may also help to maintain social media websites and regularly analyze social media analytics. This position requires strong writing skills, a broad knowledge of social media platforms and analytics, and creative campaign planning abilities. Social media coordinators and managers should also be familiar with search engine marketing (SEM) and search engine optimization (SEO) strategies.

Community Marketing Coordinator or Manager

Community marketing coordinators or managers (depending on level of experience) help to grow brand awareness within specific markets through community engagement strategies. This job requires research to identify and engage community partnership opportunities, strong social media engagement and management, and excellent interpersonal communication skills.

INSIDER INSIGHT

TONYA HOTTMANN, DIRECTOR OF MARKETING

What is your job description?

I am a director of marketing, with an emphasis on digital marketing, for a global telecommunications company. My responsibilities include website building, e-commerce, SEO and SEM, display advertising, campaign development, and marketing automation. I have managed a variety of talented people in all of these disciplines.

Describe a day in the life of your job.

Every day is different, but two common areas apply daily: (1) meetings and (2) e-mails. Every day starts and ends with both, and they fill up a significant portion of my day. Currently, I manage a variety of agencies for digital marketing all with different skill levels, expertise, and backgrounds. Building consensus and agreement are key areas when dealing with projects that span several lines of business and a variety of stakeholders, so part of my days are spent getting alignment. In digital marketing it is crucial to keep up with the latest trends and changes so I am always reading and researching to stay up to date.

What are the biggest misconceptions about your industry?

I think the biggest misconception about marketing in general is that anyone can do it. Marketing is a combination of art and science. Digital marketing requires strong communication skills as well as deep analytical capabilities. It also requires the ability to learn complex systems such as marketing automation tools, various advertising platforms, and analytic systems. It isn't just designing a pretty picture. It is what impacts what, the effect of the impact, and how we maximize our efforts to achieve our goals. It requires a daily commitment to analyzing, testing and re-creating to get results.

What is the best professional advice you have received?

- Consensus building is critical.
- Not everyone will like you, but you need to earn respect.
- Set daily goals, and always work to achieve them.
- Learn to prioritize. Not everything is urgent or crucial.

How have mentors influenced your career?

I've been fortunate to have several wise sages as mentors. From them, I have learned new digital marketing skills, communication tactics with people from a variety of disciplines, negotiation practices, and how to build consensus.

What are a few things you wish you had learned in school about your career?

Everything! When I went to college (many years ago), we didn't have the Internet. Now, I cannot imagine life without it. I started out with a BBA in marketing and an MBA in finance and decision sciences/statistics. Digital marketing requires good writing skills, mathematical capabilities, and technical proficiencies. A great digital marketer has all three.

What do you love about working in your industry?

It is ever-changing and growing. It is fast-paced, which I find very exciting.

What do you think are emerging trends within your industry?

In digital marketing, there are several including the explosion of mobile, rise in voice search, Internet, speed of video adaption, and in-app advertising, just to name a few.

(Continued)

(Continued)

What advice do you have for someone starting out in your industry?

- Practice writing skills daily.
- Take advantage of advanced analytics courses. You'll need them.
- Stay on top of trends.
- Learn emerging technologies.

What are the three most essential skills for success in your industry?

1. Good writing skills
2. Mathematical capabilities and/or analytics
3. Technical proficiencies

How has networking influenced your professional life?

Networking is very important for those starting out in marketing and those currently in the field. I have hired people through networking and been hired myself through it. I have learned new skills, discovered new trends, and been exposed to a variety of industries.

What professional groups do you belong to, and how do those influence your career?

I have belonged to several "in person" professional groups in the past, including the Chartered Institute of Management Accountants (CIMA) and the Information Technology Alliance (ITA). Right now, my professional groups are all through LinkedIn, which cover a variety of digital marketing and marketing automation groups.

How do you suggest someone stay up to date on your industry and remain competitive?

Read daily, and attend webinars on new topics. Some of my favorite reads are Moz (https://moz.com), Search Engine Land (https://searchengineland.com), Marketing Land (https://marketingland.com), Google Blog (https://www.blog.google), Google Developers Forum (https://developers.google.com/google-apps/sites/forum), and eMarketer (https://www.emarketer.com).

ADVERTISING AND MARKETING JOBS: BY THE NUMBERS

Annual median pay in 2014 for managers

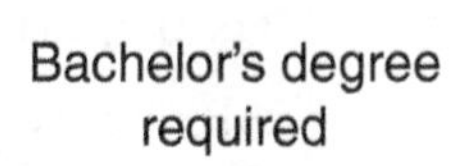

225,200 jobs in 2014

19,700 more jobs by 2024

Job outlook is 9% faster than average.

Source: Adapted from the U.S. Bureau of Labor Statistics (2017a).

SKILLS NEEDED FOR ADVERTISING AND MARKETING

The following list highlights some of the top skills needed for careers in advertising and marketing. This is not a comprehensive list. Some jobs may require additional skills not listed here.

- Ability to multitask
- Analysis skills
- Bachelor's degree
- Creative thinking
- Design experience (Adobe)
- Detail-oriented
- HTML
- Interpersonal communication
- Organized
- Research
- Teamwork
- Writing

JOB SEARCH TERMS

These are some job searching terms that can be used to help you find advertising and marketing jobs. This is not a comprehensive list—just a way to help you get started. Keep in mind that entry-level jobs are those that require a college degree with 1 to 3 years of experience. Internship experience can count toward that.

Advertising Search Terms

Account coordinator

Advertising associate or assistant

Advertising coordinator

Copywriter

Creative assistant

Entry-level advertising

Production assistant

Marketing Search Terms

Copy editor

Entry-level marketing

Marketing analyst

Marketing associate or assistant

Marketing coordinator

Marketing research assistant

Social media coordinator

PUBLIC RELATIONS

Public relations (PR) is often referred to as a "thankless" profession, despite the hard work, long hours, and ruthless dedication the industry requires for success. It is considered thankless because as a PR professional, you are helping to get media attention, plan events, and tell the stories of other people and companies. When you pitch a story to a news outlet, the journalist gets the byline, and the client gets the spotlight; you get nothing other than the satisfaction (and the paycheck) for obtaining the attention. So, while PR is often portrayed as glamorous, fast-paced, and full of "it" people, the true PR professionals often go quietly unnoticed.

WHAT IS PUBLIC RELATIONS?

PR tends to be defined in various ways, depending on the source. However, the Public Relations Society of America (PRSA; 2012) surveyed its members and conducted extensive research to formulate a succinct and accurate definition: "Public relations is a strategic communication process that builds mutually beneficial relationships between an organization and their publics." The semantics aside, there are six defining characteristics of public relations that will remain as definitions continue to evolve over time: deliberate, planned, performance, public interest, two-way communication, and management function (Wilcox, Cameron, & Reber, 2015). PR is an intentional activity designed to influence and gain understanding, provide information, and obtain feedback. Thus, PR is deliberate. PR requires organized, systematic thinking that requires research. Therefore, PR is planned. Effective PR is based on policies and performance. PR will not generate goodwill if the organization has poor policies or is unresponsive to their publics. PR is driven by public interest, and PR activity should be mutually beneficial to the organization and the public. In order to generate goodwill and serve the public, PR must use two-way communication tactics. PR is more than just disseminating information; it is also the art of listening and engaging with diverse groups. Finally, PR is the most effective when it is a strategic part of top management to help the organization reach their goals.

To understand what PR is, one must also understand what PR is not. The field of PR has suffered from many unflattering terms and stereotypes, which has negatively influenced the industry and the expectations of those trying to break into the field. For example, PR is often portrayed as a glamorous career filled with parties and event planning. While event planning can be a fruitful career path, it is not glamorous. In fact, CareerCast (2017) ranks the role of event planner as the sixth most stressful job in America. PR executive, in seventh place, closely follows it. Another misconception is that PR offers the opportunity to be a publicist or press agent. However, the reality is that outside of Hollywood and glamorized politics, these roles rarely exist within mainstream PR (Wilcox et al., 2015). Both of these misconceptions (event planners and publicists) are due in large part to the unrealistic portrayals of PR on television and within mainstream media.

PR also has some very negative stereotypes that are perpetuated by mass media. If you were to ask a PR practitioner how they "spin" information, you'd likely receive a curt response since practitioners are not in the business of spinning information. PR spin has a negative connotation, inferring that the field is not trustworthy or transparent and twists the facts. In reality, both PR practitioners and journalists engage in "framing," which is a more ethical approach to disseminating information. PR practitioners are encouraged and expected to be strict advocates for their organization, but the PRSA Code of Ethics also strictly encourages and enforces honesty within the practice. Similar to spin, the term *flack* also has a long history with PR. Flack, similar to calling a journalist a "hack," was used as a synonym for "press agent" in the 1930s and 1940s (Wilcox et al., 2015).

The mass media, particularly journalists, can be credited with coining the concept of "PR stunt," another misconception of the practice of PR. A PR stunt is essentially "the art of saying nothing" (Wilcox et al., 2015, p. 11) or garnering attention using unethical or misleading methods with the goal of increased promotion. Unfortunately, this is a problem across all areas of mass communication and not relegated to PR. Incompetence occurs in all fields, but good practitioners do not have to rely on these tactics to reach their goals.

HISTORY OF PUBLIC RELATIONS

Perhaps the idea of PR stunts has a much earlier inception with the pseudo-event created by P. T. Barnum (Wilcox et al., 2015). You may recognize the Barnum name because it is associated with the Ringling Bros. and Barnum & Bailey Circus. A pseudo-event is a planned happening that occurs primarily for the purpose of being reported (Wilcox et al., 2015). Barnum was notorious for using exaggeration, controversy, and heavy publicity to promote his entertainment attractions. He is credited with creating Tom Thumb, one of America's first media celebrities (Wilcox et al., 2015). Thumb was a 2-foot-tall, 15-pound man with exceptional singing, dancing, and comedic abilities. It was through Tom Thumb that Barnum created "third-party endorsements," a tactic still commonly used today.

Although PR has roots within the 1800s and the 19th century, it is the first 50 years of the 20th century where the true PR pioneers emerged. Ivy Lee and Edward Bernays (remember him from Chapter 2?) are considered the two outstanding pioneers of the industry (Wilcox et al., 2015). Ivy Lee opened his first PR firm, Parker and Lee, in 1905 and was hired as the "publicity counselor" to the Pennsylvania Railroad. When a railroad accident occurred, rather than keep the press out, which had been the norm to date, Lee invited the press to the scene of the accident for reporting. This was a revolutionary strategy and is credited as the beginning of an open information policy between PR and the press (Wilcox et al., 2015). Throughout the rest of his career, Lee successfully decreased public opposition on behalf of several companies, including the Rockefeller Family, which was arguably his most well-known work. Today, Lee is remembered for making four main contributions to PR: (1) advancing the concept that business and industry should align themselves with public interest, (2) refusing to execute any campaign without the support of top management, (3) maintaining open communication with the news media, and (4) emphasizing the necessity of humanizing business (Wilcox et al., 2015). Other pioneers within this era include Arthur W. Page, who is credited with establishing PR as an integral part of corporate management and fashion publicist Eleanor Lambert (Wilcox et al., 2015).

After World War II, changes in American society, such as urbanization, television, and business expansion, changed the landscape of PR. It was during this time that PR shifted away from being solely media relations and began to include reputation management and relationship building. Maybe only coincidentally, this is also when women began to enter the field of PR (Wilcox et al., 2015). By 2000, PR had become a management function operating at the highest levels of an organization.

PUBLIC RELATIONS TODAY

Today, women account for approximately 70% of PR practitioners (Wilcox et al., 2015). Also, similar to the evolution of PR that occurred after WWII, digital advances are revolutionizing the field. There is now an increased emphasis on listening, engagement, and dialogue with publics, specifically online (Wilcox et al., 2015). PR is also still evolving into a field of relationship management, building upon the ideas of excellence theory and two-way symmetrical communication. Two-way symmetrical communication is increasingly easier with digital communication advances.

Digital advances have also reduced cultural barriers and created a more multicultural world for practicing PR. For example, we can now connect quickly with people in other countries, and our messages reach an international audience more than ever before. While previous PR practices encouraged cultural sensitivity, they often also used different strategies and tactics for various cultural audiences. Today, PR must integrate cultural knowledge into one strategy to cultivate a more holistic approach to practicing PR and disseminating information (Wilcox et al., 2015). Similar to the increased attention to multicultural audiences is a greater need to recruit minorities into the PR workforce. The ideal workforce in PR would more closely reflect the diverse U.S. population. Specifically, there is a strong need to recruit Hispanics because they are the fastest growing U.S. population, according to the U.S. Census Bureau (2017). African Americans and Asians are also growing populations and should be more strategically recruited into PR roles. A driving factor of the lack of a diverse PR workforce is the lack of diversity within college PR programs, indicating that recruitment needs to begin during college rather than workforce entry.

Another trend of PR that will continue for years to come is the public's demand for transparency as the role of PR continues to expand. Understanding that PR is now more than just media relations and publicity, more active leadership and engagement with the public is needed. Showing ownership and value of branding, relationship building, and positioning efforts is essential to the continued growth and success of PR. Integrated communications campaigns that work harmoniously with marketing and advertising can help build transparent relationships with diverse publics and help consumers feel like engaged stakeholders, rather than pawns in a marketing scheme. Further, everything a company says and does is now up for public debate and discourse. Creating corporate social responsibility (CSR) programs can shift the agenda of conversation to more positive areas of business while simultaneously demonstrating the value of PR for goodwill.

Lastly, an increased emphasis on measurement and evaluation, coupled with increased and lifelong professional development, are two more trends in today's PR industry. Again, thanks to digital advances, a stronger emphasis is needed on measurement and evaluation. This can be challenging due to the speed at which things are changing. However, through engagement with groups such as PRSA, practitioners can come together to share ideas and brainstorm effective measurement and evaluation techniques for more complex and integrated campaigns. An important measurement is the return on investment (ROI) to show value to top management and gain credibility for future campaigns. Two other important measurement dimensions are measuring outcomes, or the long-term effectiveness of a program, and measuring outputs, or how well a campaign was executed and how effective the tactics were (Wilcox et al., 2015).

CAREERS IN PUBLIC RELATIONS

Careers in PR are divided into two types: (1) agency or firm or (2) in-house work. It is often very difficult for those starting out in PR to know which one is right for them. However, choosing in-house or agency work is not a lifelong commitment.

Many practitioners switch between agencies and organizations depending on their specialties and the cultural fit. When choosing which is right for you, take special consideration of each position's unique responsibilities while also thinking about the types of clients and people you want to work with and the type of environment you want to work in.

The role of PR within an organization (not a PR firm or agency) is dependent upon the type of organization, the perceptions of top management, and the capabilities of the PR executive (Wilcox et al., 2015). Typically, someone with a director or vice president job title manages in-house PR teams. For example, a vice president of corporate communications might oversee PR, marketing, and advertising communications. Some organizations also have a chief communications officer (CCO) who helps manage and lead internal PR teams. In-house teams range in size, but on average, Fortune 500 companies have about 24 people working in PR/corporate communications roles (USC Annenberg, 2007). Smaller businesses have fewer PR employees, ranging from 1 to 10 PR practitioners (Wilcox et al., 2015). The U.S. Bureau of Labor Statistics (2017b) reports that PR salaries range from $32,000 to $110,000 with a median salary of $58,000.

Working within an organization practicing PR also requires cooperation with other staff functions, including legal, human resources (HR), advertising, and marketing. However, some in-house teams are moving toward outsourcing some projects. The biggest reason that organizations outsource PR work is to bring in expertise and resources that cannot be found internally (Wilcox et al., 2015). The most frequently outsourced activities are writing and communications, media relations, publicity, strategy and planning, and event planning (Wilcox et al., 2015). While outsourcing can be beneficial for the workload of organizations, it can also lead to employee dissatisfaction and long-term resentment if the reasons for hiring are not communicated effectively with in-house employees.

PR firms or agencies provide a variety of services, including marketing communications, executive speech writing or training, research and evaluation, crisis communication, media analysis, community relations, events management, public affairs, branding and corporate reputation, and financial relations. However, not every firm does every thing. Most firms specialize in one area such as crisis communication, or like Alexandra in the Insider Insight. Conversely, Evan's firm focuses more heavily on marketing and PR campaigns within the local community for nonprofit and for profit clients. If you have a very specific area of interest or expertise, working in an agency might be ideal for you. However, agency work also requires great flexibility and adaptability because all clients are not created equal. You may have to quickly shift from working on writing to media relations, back to writing, and then to event planning all within the same workday and possibly for varying industries depending on your clientele.

PUBLIC RELATIONS DUTIES

Whether you work in an agency or in-house, as a PR practitioner you can expect to execute various activities. PR practitioners typically do the following (U.S. Bureau of Labor Statistics, 2017b):

- Write news releases and prepare information for the media
- Identify main client groups and audiences and determine the best way to reach them
- Respond to media requests for information
- Designate an appropriate spokesperson to deliver information
- Help clients communicate effectively with the public
- Develop and maintain corporate images and identities using logos and signs
- Draft speeches and arrange interviews for top leadership
- Evaluate advertising and promotion programs to determine whether or not they are compatible with PR efforts
- Develop and carry out fund-raising strategies by identifying and contacting potential donors and applying for grants

INSIDER INSIGHT

EVAN S. K. SULLIVAN, APR, DIRECTOR OF PUBLIC RELATIONS (AGENCY)

Describe a day in the life of your job.

The excitement of this job is that every day is different—as cliché as that sounds. I spend most of the day writing, which can be everything from drafting newsletters, to crafting social media posts, e-mails, and copy.

In between, I maintain relationships in the community and with reporters. Managing client expectations is where most of my time goes.

What are the biggest misconceptions about your industry?

I'm always surprised how glamorized the industry is. The misconception that we are all living a *Devil Wears Prada*, Samantha from *Sex and the City* lifestyle makes me laugh but also hurts our industry and credibility. I am not sipping champagne for breakfast, lunch, and dinner. Coffee, however, that's another story.

What is the best professional advice you have received?

Slow down. News moves fast, PR moves fast, but mistakes happen if you aren't taking the time to review. There may be a solution or idea in the space you've given yourself to pause.

What are a few things you wish you had learned in school about your career?

I don't know many PR curriculums that really share how much time you spend on pitching and, even more, how to keep at getting a story placed. It can take time.

Sometimes you feel like the preteen girl waiting at the door for someone to come to your party. You are crossing your fingers and toes that the cool kids want to hang out with you. When they do, it is really amazing! When they don't, you have to pick yourself up and reinvent yourself and develop thicker skin. Nobody likes to hear no.

What do you love about working in your industry?

I love being able to help others tell their stories—being able to articulate their passion and business stories so they can achieve their business goals.

What do you think are emerging trends within your industry?

I believe digital media clearly has changed the delivery of content. I can't imagine this not evolving. I do believe that we have a responsibility to look at our client's goals and think about how we can holistically achieve these. It may be through digital, advertising, earned media or community partnerships and placements. I am a big believer in cross-channel approaches and the integration of "new" with "old."

What advice do you have for someone starting out in your industry?

Put in the work. Roll up your sleeves, and volunteer to help or observe. I am most impressed and inspired by those who show the initiative to learn and hustle to learn. I've done way more than collating presentations and building media lists. My daily work has included everything from inflating giant pool floats, folding bras, to directing mascots, building centerpieces, and assembling my own trade show booths.

What are the three most essential skills for success in your industry?

1. It is essential to look at the big picture and think of the long game. Strategy is what sets apart a technician and why a client would come to you.

(Continued)

(Continued)

Without strategy, there can be little accountability, measurement, and understanding of how the budget is getting used.

2. While PR is about relationships, I believe having an understanding of the editorial and writing process is important. Being able to find the news hook and craft a clean, clear message is essential.
3. If we are overwhelmed by messages and images and stories every second, you can imagine how many e-mails and calls reporters get. You have to be willing to work to get your story told and to work new angles to get the story through the noise pollution. You can't give up. You have to hustle to make connections. Think of a unique perspective and connect with the audience. Having the tenacity to keep at it is really important.

How has networking influenced your professional life?

There is tremendous power in relationships. Connecting the dots between different groups and taking advantage of acquaintances, memberships, friendships, and professional connections is a big part of PR.

I found my last two positions through networking. I recommend getting involved in volunteering, professional groups, and special interest groups to make connections and showing what skills you bring to the table. You never know what will come of it.

What professional groups do you belong to, and how do those influence your career?

I am a member of the Public Relations Society of America (PRSA) and have been a member of the International Association of Business Communicators. Membership in these organizations allows me to stay on top of trends, learn from peers, and has helped me network.

I received my national accreditation from PRSA (Accreditation in Public Relations, or APR) in 2015. This has been a positive seal of approval of my skills.

Volunteering with the local PRSA chapter has introduced me to peers to bounce ideas off of and learn from while developing leadership skills.

How do you suggest someone stay up to date on your industry and remain competitive?

Read. Keep up with news and how you get your news. This will point you in the direction of not only industry trends but also how the consumption of your news is influenced. I am a news junkie.

INSIDER INSIGHT

ALEXANDRA SABBAG, FOUNDER AND PRINCIPAL

What is your job description?

I am the owner of a small communications company in Chicago, specializing in fund-raising and PR for nonprofit organizations (NPOs). Given we are a small business, my role varies between in-house council, to accountant, to human resources (HR), and everything in between. I manage client relationships, develop program strategy, and coordinate strategic partnerships, to name a few.

Describe a day in the life of your job.

I don't have a typical day. My day is dictated almost entirely by client needs. I typically start my day in the office and finish with meetings or a yoga class to clear my mind. When I am in the office, I am constantly updating our clients with project benchmarks or meeting with my team to understand where we are on various programs.

What are the biggest misconceptions about your industry?

The biggest misconception, for my role specifically, is that my calendar is packed with fund-raisers and parties. We attend each fund-raising event on behalf of our clients, but beyond that, my calendar stays relatively free from formal commitments.

What is the best professional advice you have received?

Never let them see you sweat. My mentor told me this early on when I was running a fund-raiser with a million moving parts. As the planner or project manager, you see it all—the good, the bad, and the ugly. The best thing you can do is keep moving forward. Recognize the issues, create a correction plan for the future, but in the moment, keep producing and keep your cool.

How have mentors influenced your career?

I knew the media and PR business when I started my company. I have always been a media relations expert and loved that part about this career. Once it was clear that AM Consulting's clientele was going to be NPOs, I made a point to pay attention to the development side of the organization. My mentor taught me the business of fund-raising, and it's a skill I continue to fine-tune

(Continued)

(Continued)

throughout my career. If sustainability is the key to success, then expertise in fund-raising is critical to the future of my company.

What are a few things you wish you had learned in school about your career?

I wish I had had more access to the real world of PR when I was in school. Relevant case studies about more than just big consumer packaged goods would have been so helpful to see the variety of PR practitioner opportunities that exist.

What do you love about working in your industry?

I have been and will continue to be dedicated to the story. A PR professional doesn't just publicize what their client tells them is news but rather digs in and collects every single detail in order to build an impactful message that communicates more than just a punchy headline.

What do you think are emerging trends within your industry?

From virally spreading news to digital fund-raising techniques, social communities inevitably offer the opportunity to reach and engage a variety of audiences.

What advice do you have for someone starting out in your industry?

Understand that you have no experience but be confident in your skill set. Perhaps you've written a few press releases or done things here and there, but adjust your mind-set to focus on why you want to work at a particular firm or for a specific company and not so much what you have done during your college career. Answer with confidence why you want to work at this place. What about them leverages your passion and makes you want to go above and beyond for them? Your heart will get you the position, and the skills you built over time will ultimately start garnering actual real-world experience that is directly in line with your passion.

What are the three most essential skills for success in your industry?

1. Kindness and willingness to do whatever it takes goes a very long way.
2. Put the time in, learn from your mistakes, and take ownership over your own career.
3. You have to be a good writer to make it. No exceptions.

How has networking influenced your professional life?

I have lived in Chicago for 13 years and have built a robust network of people across a variety of industries and disciplines. The better you know someone and the more often you see them, the easier and more natural it is to ask them for something.

How do you suggest someone stay up to date on your industry and remain competitive?

My business grew and achieved success by the work we did for our clients. I was dedicated, passionate, and worked tirelessly until the job was done. Focus on producing the best possible product and let the work speak for itself.

INSIDER INSIGHT

ERIN SPAIN, COMMUNICATIONS DIRECTOR

What is your job description?

I am the communications director at Northwestern University Feinberg School of Medicine. I lead a team that produces compelling content to promote research and education activities at the medical school.

This includes developing long- and short-term strategic communication plans and creating or managing the creation of content such as monthly newsletters, videos, social media campaigns, website content, e-mail communication, flyers, advertisements, brochures, and more.

Other duties include organizing major research- and education-related events on campus such as our annual research day, where students, faculty, and residents showcase their work in a poster session along with a keynote speaker event and an awards program.

Describe a day in the life of your job.

My day starts on my iPhone during my bus commute to work. I check, respond to, and send e-mails and organize my calendar for the day. I also check our social media accounts and engage with our followers.

When I arrive at work, I spend another hour responding to e-mails and scheduling meetings and follow-ups and then turning my attention to the projects of the day. This might include a few hours in InDesign working on newsletter layout, copyediting stories written by our content creators, reviewing social media plans for upcoming events, or advising colleagues who have communications-related requests.

(Continued)

(Continued)

I have one-on-one meetings with each member of my team once a week. I organize their assignments in an online project management tool and review their work on a daily basis.

I also work closely with the university media relations team and communications team from our affiliate hospitals to pitch story ideas, share new initiatives, and make sure our brand efforts are being enforced.

What are the biggest misconceptions about your industry?

Easy access to tools used by professional communicators such as HD and digital cameras, online content development tools, and social media leads some to think that anyone with a computer and phone can successfully drive communication efforts for an organization. This is not true.

In my industry, we tell complicated stories about medical breakthroughs in a compelling, consistent way that promotes the goals of the institution. I work closely with our leadership team to refine the messages that tell our story. I have to be a creative problem solver who handles a variety of assignments such as writing talking points for a brilliant scientist who is about to speak to a room of VIPs, to copyediting a 14-page newsletter in AP style, and selecting and prepping representatives of our organization for a big-budget video shoot. This takes skill, experience, and a strategic approach that doesn't come bundled with the latest piece of technology.

What is the best professional advice you have received?

Ask for the promotion, ask for the raise, and ask for the tools you need to do your job better. If you don't speak up, you will miss out.

How have mentors influenced your career?

My mentors have been my biggest cheerleaders. They have confidence in my abilities and offer advice when I face difficult professional situations. They are well connected and have opened doors within their professional networks to help me build my career.

What are a few things you wish you had learned in school about your career?

You never stop learning. Technology and trends change quickly in communication. You need to keep learning to keep your skills up to date, or you will be looked over or will fall behind.

What do you love about working in your industry?

It is very fulfilling to be surrounded by extremely intelligent people and have the ability to help them explain their work to a lay audience.

What do you think are emerging trends within your industry?

Everyone is using his or her phone to communicate, and our content needs to be as mobile-friendly as possible.

What advice do you have for someone starting out in your industry?

- Never skip the chance to learn a new skill.
- Master the Adobe Creative Suite, shadow the staff photographer, and hold their bag or tripod and observe them working.
- Offer to assist with event planning and any other opportunity that comes along that is beyond the scope of your job.
- Build your skills by inserting yourself into new situations.
- Once you become a known, reliable member of the team, who is pleasant and willing to help, doors will open and your career will take off!

What are the three most essential skills for success in your industry?

1. Be responsive. If you leave e-mails, phone calls, or requests unanswered, you hurt your reputation as an effective communicator. If you don't know how to respond to something, let the person know that you will get back to them shortly. Acknowledging their request gives you instant credibility.
2. Come up with creative solutions. Budgets are small and expectations can be big, and creative problem-solving is often the best way to please your client. Repurpose or refresh existing content or assets; reach out to your network for help. There are often low or no cost solutions right in front of you if you're being creative.
3. Be kind and assertive at the same time. You shouldn't have to be unkind or rude to do your job. It takes experience and effort, but a polished, professional person can deal with difficult situations without losing their cool.

How has networking influenced your professional life?

My last two career moves have been a direct result of connections within my professional network. An impressive résumé can get your foot in the door, but if the hiring manager hears a positive personal endorsement about a candidate from someone they know, your chances of getting hired skyrocket!

(Continued)

(Continued)

How do you suggest someone stay up to date on your industry and remain competitive?

- Follow brands and organizations you admire, and watch what they are doing and learn from their attempts.
- Read as much as you can in newspapers, blogs, and on social media posts about trends.
- Don't let your skills get rusty. I was a video producer in a previous job, and I make sure to edit a video or two a year to make sure I still understand the software and can keep that skill in my arsenal. I am a managing editor of several publications, but twice a year I also write feature stories to be sure I have fresh content with my byline.

PUBLIC RELATIONS JOBS: BY THE NUMBERS

Annual median pay in 2016 for PR professionals

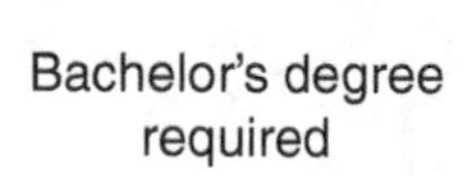

240,700 jobs in 2014

14,900 more jobs by 2024

Most PR professionals work more than 40 hours per week.

Source: Adapted from the U.S. Bureau of Labor Statistics (2017b).

SKILLS NEEDED FOR PUBLIC RELATIONS

Depending on your specific role within PR, your career may require more of these skills than others. However, a basic understanding and ability to execute the following skills at the entry-level stage of a PR career are essential. Additional skills that can help you succeed within the field are intellectual curiosity, knowledge of PR theory, exceptional communication skills, cultural competence, a strong work ethic, and the ability to efficiently multitask (Commission on Public Relations Education, 2015).

Business competence
Planning
Problem-solving
Research
Social media
Writing

JOB SEARCH TERMS

Depending on where you are applying, PR may live under a different term. What follows are some of the additional ways PR is identified in various organizations to help jump-start your job search.

Communications
Corporate communications
Development
Employee relations
Entry-level public relations
Financial relations
Government affairs
Issues management
Media relations
Public affairs
Public information
Public relations

JOURNALISM

Think about how your friends would describe you for a minute: Would they say that you're a news junkie? Someone who is addicted to writing? A person who can't help talking to other people and figuring out their story? If any of these remotely describe you, then you already have some of the essential skills for a career in journalism. If you are dedicated to finding the truth, enjoy research and writing, and have a passion for sharing information, read on about careers in journalism.

WHAT IS JOURNALISM?

Journalism is the activity of gathering, assessing, creating, and presenting news and information. It is also the product of these activities (American Press Institute, 2016). Journalism has several defining characteristics that set it apart from other forms of communication and other industries. First, journalism is news and is seen as more valuable than other "noise" we encounter on a daily basis. The news value of journalism is rooted within the goals of journalism: to provide people with verified information they can use to make better decisions (American Press Institute, 2016). Second, journalism is a systematic process that requires journalists to not only find the facts but also the truth about the facts (American Press Institute, 2016). This is often referred to as objectivity. Third, the purpose of journalism is unique. Kovach and Rosenstiel (2007) explain that advances in technology and the use of sophisticated methods do not define journalism, unlike other mass communication industries. Rather, the guiding purpose of journalism, the role that news plays in our daily lives is what defines journalism as an industry.

There are many elements to journalism—the first and foremost being the truth. Just as consumers seek truth in advertising and marketing, they also rely on the news and newsmakers (journalists) to present reliable, accurate facts. Journalism employs "journalistic truth," which is a process beginning with professional discipline to assemble and verify pieces of information. Then, journalists try to convey that information in a meaningful and accurate format for readers

(Kovach & Rosenstiel, 2007). This requires journalists to be transparent about their research methods so that audiences can easily verify and seek additional information as needed. The journalistic truth also requires that journalism's first loyalty is to citizens. Similar to public relations (PR), journalists must strive to put the public interest above their own self-interest or assumptions (Kovach & Rosenstiel, 2007). Many variables such as ethnocentrism, political bias, social order, and individualism can contaminate the ability for a journalist to be objective (Vivian, 2011). However, the most successful journalists will master their objectivity in order to uphold the standards within the industry.

In essence, journalism is a discipline of verification. It is impossible for a journalist to be entirely objective, but journalistic methods can and should be entirely objective (Kovach & Rosenstiel, 2007). Methods such as seeking out multiple witnesses, disclosing as much as possible about sources, or presenting both sides of an issue signify objectivity in research methods. This is one element of journalism that sets the industry apart from others, like marketing or advertising, where there is not the same standard for objective research and reporting. In addition to research methods, independence is a cornerstone of reliability (Kovach & Rosenstiel, 2007). Journalists must not be swayed by sources or power or by their own self-interest. Journalists must operate with an open mind and intellectual curiosity. However, independence is not synonymous with neutrality. The source of credibility is a journalist's accuracy and ability to inform, not their desire for certain outcomes or allegiance to specific groups. Therefore, journalists must avoid arrogance, elitism, and isolation (Kovach & Rosenstiel, 2007).

Finally, the industry of journalism must provide a forum for public criticism and compromise, keep the news comprehensive and proportional, and respect the news rights of citizens (Kovach & Rosenstiel, 2007). As agenda setting theory would argue, journalists help people learn what issues they should be thinking about. Therefore, the news media create an opportunity for public discussion and debate. With this ability comes great responsibility and conferred privileges, including subsidies for distribution or research and development and laws protecting content and free speech. These privileges are predicated on the fact that journalists will provide content that citizens and government need to make better choices and to be more informed (Kovach & Rosenstiel, 2007).

Journalism is purposeful storytelling and our modern cartography. We use the information journalists provide as a map to help us navigate society. Thus, journalists are tasked with providing comprehensive, relevant, and significant information. This is becoming more and more of a challenge in today's society when average people operate like journalists, often using similar methods and reaching similar audiences. Journalists must remember and stay true to their motives and intent—to give people the information they need. Journalists also must continue to produce "functional truth," as opposed to content that is simply interesting or informative, to remain significant and credible. Finally, journalists, unlike other content creators, have a responsibility to help people understand what information matters, why, and how it may affect their lives (American Press Institute, 2016).

HISTORY OF JOURNALISM

U.S. journalism has evolved through four distinctive eras: (1) the colonial, (2) partisan, (3) penny, and (4) yellow press periods. The first newspaper, *Publick Occurrences*, debuted in Boston in 1690 by Benjamin Harris (Vivian, 2011). This publication alleged that the King of France had spent special time with his son's wife. However, because this information was published without the required royal consent, Harris was out of business before the next issue. Shortly after Harris's attempt at creating a newspaper, John Peter Zenger started the *New York Weekly Journal*, supported by people who disliked the royal governor. Zenger was later arrested for his publication and put to a historic trial where he was supported and subsequently freed (Vivian, 2011). Zenger's success led to other journalism advancements, and today, many traditions established in the colonial era remain. For example, the news media still deeply value their independence from government censorship, and seek the truth no matter the implications.

The partisan press era, also known as the Federalist period in U.S. history, saw a shift in journalism based on party lines. It was during this period that the *Federalist Papers* were published throughout the nation (Vivian, 2011). The partisanship only intensified after the Constitution was drafted, which led to the creation of the Alien and Sedition Acts, prohibiting journalists from making any false, scandalous, or malicious statements about the government. Finally, Thomas Jefferson was elected president, and the Federalists were kicked out of office. This era is the reason why the government keeps their hands off of the press (for the most part) today and also why the news media serve as a forum for debate (Vivian, 2011).

The *Sun* was printed in 1833 and sold for a penny per copy—hence, the penny press era. During this period, the telegraph was invented, editorials were printed, the speed of news coverage improved, and the inverted pyramid style of writing was born (Vivian, 2011). The penny press era is arguably the most influential era of journalism. Building upon the advances of the penny press era, the yellow press period introduced stunt journalism and sensationalism. The "yellow kid" was a popular cartoon character in New York newspapers during this time and represented the fabrication used by journalists to grab the attention of readers. We can credit the yellow period for today's tabloid magazines, websites, and dramatized documentary television programming.

JOURNALISM TODAY

Today, the journalism industry is characterized by new realities and trends. For example, think about how you receive your news versus how your parents get their news. Are there differences? Likely, yes. Thanks to technological advances, younger people receive more of their news from online sources, rather than print or television mediums. The trends of cyber news and aggregate news have changed the landscape of the traditional newsroom. There is now less enterprise, less comprehensive coverage, and fewer beats. Web news is popular because it is relatively low-cost to implement but can generate high levels of revenue from advertising. Aggregate and cyber news sites are also free to the consumer, as opposed to a newspaper or cable subscription, and often provide more comprehensive coverage in part due to the interactive nature through comments. Two of the biggest and most popular cyber news aggregate websites are the *Drudge Report* and the *HuffPost* (Vivian, 2011).

We experience nonstop coverage of news, which is a benefit for the audience but often a challenge for journalists. This puts the journalists, reporters, and editors under immense pressure. Especially for more tenured journalists, the 24/7 news cycle is a major change from having one deadline per day. Now, the deadlines are seemingly endless and immediate. Although audiences favor the nonstop coverage, the quality of reporting has suffered. It is now more common to read news stories that include typos, since there are fewer editors overseeing more reporters with a much tighter schedule. Also, the 24/7 news cycle creates competition for reporters to be first and break the news but also sacrifices the time they have to put together thoughtful, compelling, and complete stories (Vivian, 2011). Moreover, viewers often see more raw footage that can appear disorganized because networks and reporters want to be showing live developments. This has led to false reports and jarring scenes. For example, NPR and other major networks originally reported a gunman in Tucson, Arizona, killed Congresswoman Gabby Giffords in 2011 only to later retract their statements when Giffords survived (Shepard, 2011). Those pursuing careers in journalism should understand the never-ending news cycle and prepare to work under tight deadlines in tense situations.

Bloggers have created a new niche and conceptualization of news. A blog is defined as "an amateur website, generally personal in nature, and often focused on a narrow subject" (Vivian, 2011, p. 234). Blogs are every bit as accessible as new sites and are often used as sources by traditional reporters. Organizations are also turning to bloggers to act as brand representatives and ambassadors through partnerships where bloggers editorialize and humanize products and services. Blogging can be categorized as "soft news" or news that is geared toward satisfying an audience's information wants rather than needs (Vivian, 2011). However, the blogging industry does not face the same regulations or privileges as journalism but can bring in equal, if not greater, revenue than aggregate websites. Whether or not blogging is a viable form of journalism is part of an ongoing, contemporary debate, but for the purposes of this text, blogging can be one avenue for a young journalist to begin a fulfilling career.

CAREERS IN JOURNALISM

The U.S. Bureau of Labor Statistics (2017c) estimates that the job outlook for reporters, correspondents, and news analysts is declining, due in large part to dips in advertising revenue. However, as people change their consumption habits, new jobs arise. For 2016, the average salary for broadcast news analysts was $56,000, and reporters and correspondents made approximately $37,000 per year (U.S. Bureau of Labor Statistics, 2017c). Journalism is an interesting industry because although it has unique careers, it also provides opportunities for people who want to work in multiple industries simultaneously, such as advertising and journalism. For example, journalism requires advertising, sales, and marketing to be effective. Therefore, if you are a person who is passionate about the journalism industry, but not interested in being a journalist, you can still find a career here. The career opportunities presented in what follows, however, are relegated to people who wish to be journalists of some sort.

Broadcast Journalist or Reporter

A broadcast journalist or reporter is responsible for delivering the news in one of many formats including radio, television, and online (i.e., podcasts). Some broadcast reporters and journalists write their own copy, while others read pre-written copy in a live setting. Also, some journalists and reporters are responsible for finding, pitching, creating, and disseminating their own stories, while others are assigned stories from an editor. You can read the Insider Insight of Natalie Brunell, a news reporter for the Sacramento NBC affiliate, later in this chapter.

Foreign Correspondent

The career of a foreign correspondent was first initiated by Ernest Hemingway through his coverage of the Spanish Civil War and WWII for several American and Canadian newspapers. Foreign correspondents present their stories almost immediately using various media channels including television, magazines, and online outlets. Foreign correspondents should be inherently curious people who are passionate about traveling and telling the stories of other cultural natives.

Freelance Writer

Freelance writing is one of the best ways for a young journalist to build up their portfolio and gain journalism experience. One benefit of freelance writing is that you act as your own boss; however, this does require significant self-discipline. Freelance writers usually specialize in one area, such as travel or food, for example. Larger publications often rely on freelance writers to provide engaging content. Freelance writers may also pitch their content to publications, much like a PR professional does. Successful careers as a freelance writer require strong writing skills, a desire to write, and determination.

Investigative Journalist

Investigative journalists are motivated by seeking the truth and gathering the reasoning for things. Investigative journalism requires patience, exceptional research skills, and a certain amount of skepticism. An understanding of the law and ethics is also especially useful. Showcasing your investigative journalism skills online through social media or writing a blog is a great way to get started and gain preliminary experience. Newspapers, television networks, and online publications use investigative journalists.

Newspaper Reporter

Newspaper reporters write for one or multiple publications, or as a freelancer, on projects assigned by an editor. This career does not have a typical work schedule. Rather, you work when the news is happening, which may require morning, evening, weekend, and holiday work schedules. Newspaper reporting requires research, interviewing, and feedback. Oftentimes, a story will go through several rounds of editing before it is ready to print. Newspaper reporters should also be able to take their own photos, if necessary, and be able to multitask since you will likely be managing multiple projects simultaneously.

Photojournalist

The key of photojournalism is to tell a comprehensive story through pictures. Photojournalists are inherently visual people who understand the power of imagery for communication. This career will put you at the center of events, disasters, and controversies. News photos must be timely, unbiased, and accurate representations of the news. As a photojournalist, you should be able to work in a variety of environments, meet deadlines, and have exceptional experience using photo equipment.

INSIDER INSIGHT

NATALIE BRUNELL, TELEVISION NEWS REPORTER

Describe a day in the life of your job.

I'm one of our nightside reporters, so I come in at 3:00 p.m. and go straight into an editorial meeting with our producers, writers, and web team. We discuss what's happening that day, and reporters receive story assignments. Then it's off to the races. I'm assigned a photographer and start making phone calls on a story or just jump into the action and get sent to a scene that's unfolding. I spend the next several hours gathering elements and information, interviewing as many people as I can. At about 7:00 or 8:00 p.m., I sit down to write my story and hand it off to my photographer for editing. He brings my story to life through the images we shot that day. Then we go live at 10:00 and 11:00 from the scene of our story or in the newsroom, and we're done!

(Continued)

(Continued)

What are the biggest misconceptions about your industry?

The biggest misconception about reporting is that it's a glamorous job. Your office is a live truck with very little room. I carry multiple bags with me to be prepared for any kind of news story (including weather and fires), and you have to be able to deal with a high-stress environment of short deadlines. You also have to be okay with moving around a bit when you start your career, and the smaller markets don't pay very well. Many people work for several years in different cities before making it to a top 10 or top 20 market.

What is the best professional advice you have received?

I've received lots of great tips and tricks for journalism along the way both from my schooling and from mentors. The first is *don't take anything at face value.* People lie, and that includes officials. You have to do as much research about your story as you can to know what questions to ask, and don't be afraid to ask tough questions. I also think it's important to find your voice and be yourself, and that really takes watching a lot of different programs and people in the industry and practicing your craft.

How have mentors influenced your career?

My mentors have been wonderful and include NBC 5 anchor Rob Stafford in Chicago, former anchor and current talent coach Terry Anzur in Los Angeles, and CBS 2 investigative reporter David Goldstein in Los Angeles. They have given me much-needed feedback and encouragement to grow in this business.

What are a few things you wish you had learned in school about your career?

There's nothing like going live. It's baptism by fire. Your nerves are racing, and you just slowly learn with each live shot how to formulate a concise story on the cuff with no teleprompter in front of you. It's a real skill and one that develops over time. I also wish that I knew the politics of this business. I learned that news directors are like casting agents. They have to fill a specific role, and sometimes you're not the right look and fit no matter how qualified you are.

What do you love about working in your industry?

My job is different every day. My scenery changes from fires to the front steps of the California Capitol to a snowstorm. I love that every day I know I'm going to meet new and interesting people and I will learn a lot.

What do you think are emerging trends within your industry?

DIGITAL. I think a lot of local news stations are still evolving on how to best integrate social media to the newscasts. We are adding platforms online, and reporters are expected to shoot digital videos on their phones. It's great to have more interactivity with the viewers, but the challenge is how much information you give away immediately online and what, if anything, you hold back for a newscast.

What advice do you have for someone starting out in your industry?

- Do internships and find mentors.
- SHADOW. Find out what it's really like to report or produce day to day, and then work really hard.
- Start at the bottom, volunteer for shifts other people don't want to do, and practice writing stories.
- Also, be kind to the people you meet in this industry. They move on, and you never know how they may come back in your life and help your career.

What are the three most essential skills for success in your industry?

1. Be determined. Dig for information and interviews no one has, and don't believe the first thing you hear.
2. Be creative. This is visual storytelling. You have the opportunity to bring the audience in through moving pictures and emotional interviews that you weave together like the director of a mini-feature.
3. Be kind. Newsrooms are teams. Be kind, and be aware that your mic can always be hot.

How has networking influenced your professional life?

It is always helpful to network because so many jobs in television are based on who you know. There are lots of different journalism associations you can join to meet other people in the business, and internships also help with that.

What professional groups do you belong to, and how do those influence your career?

I belong to the Association of Women Journalists, which was kind enough to grant me a scholarship while I was receiving my graduate degree in journalism at Medill, and I'm also a part of the Associated Press Television and Radio Association (APTRA). I'm also looking into joining an investigative journalism group.

How do you suggest someone stay up to date on your industry and remain competitive?

Consume the news. Read it on the web; watch it on television. The only way to know where this industry is going is to stay on top of it day to day, minute to minute.

INSIDER INSIGHT

KATEY McFARLAN, BLOGGER

What is your job description?

I got my degree in public relations (PR) from the University of Texas at Arlington. After interning in nonprofit, corporate, and agency environments, I went to work at a lifestyle PR firm in Dallas, Texas. At the time, the opinion leaders we were working with on campaigns made a shift from celebrities and traditional media to social media influencers. My job then became negotiating and implementing campaigns with those influencers. I had to make sure the brand aligned with the influencer's brand and that these would be mutually beneficial partnerships. I started a blog to research the ins and outs of the industry and started to make examples for the influencers I was working with. A little bit later on, I went full-time with my blog. Today I am the owner and content creator of Chronicles of Frivolity, a lifestyle blog based out of Texas. My job is to connect brands to readers, through brand campaigns.

Describe a day in the life of your job.

Essentially my job is to run a website and create content for my platforms daily: blog, social media, etc. I start my day with photo shoots with photographers. Campaigns and blog posts can be booked up to 6 months in advance, so we are constantly shooting product and looks that brands can approve. After shoots, I work on e-mails. My job is to respond to brands and plan out campaigns based on research I have from my readers. I have traditional research through website analytics, focus groups, surveys, and market trends. With this, we are really able to pinpoint and plan what would best help my readers and the brand at the same time. Along with responding to brands and my affiliate networks, I respond to readers. Sometimes I feel like bloggers are the "Dear Abbys" of the day, and I love it. I love that this platform allows me to help mentor girls with anything from career guidance to styling. After e-mails, I will head to Dallas to meet with either brands or my affiliate network. They connect me to different campaigns and allow me to monetize my blog. In the afternoon, I work on content. I aim to complete around two blog posts a day and finish by planning my editorial calendar. Throughout this, I make sure to keep up with social media and interact with readers so I can answer their questions. Other weeks are different; I'm in New York a lot meeting with brands I am an ambassador to, or there are always fun weeks like Fashion Week! I also make sure to attend conferences so I can stay educated on emerging trends in advertising and social media.

What are the biggest misconceptions about your industry?

I think the biggest misconception is why bloggers start their blog. Many girls e-mail me saying they love clothes so they want to start a blog. I love integrating key messaging from a brand and making sure that it serves my readers' wants. Every successful blogger I know started their blog because they loved writing, photography, hypertext markup language (HTML), advertising, PR, marketing, or social media. Most don't ever start because they just love clothes. Clothes are the medium in which we are able to connect to readers, but they aren't the message.

What is the best professional advice you have received?

"If you are asked to find an orange, and the market is only selling apples, buy the apple and paint it orange." One of my professors really instilled the idea that you can't have excuses. That saying has always stayed with me when working on deadlines or short lead times. I may think a turnaround time is impossible, but I get it done no questions asked. Campaigns are so sensitive to timelines, and I can't be the reason something got delayed.

How have mentors influenced your career?

I would say that I wish I had a mentor. With this field being so incredibly new and word-of-mouth advertising taking this industry by such a rapid pace, there aren't necessarily a lot of mentors. Blogging as a whole is very "fend for yourself and figure it out." Because of this, I host The Blog Workshop Dallas with two other industry leaders each year so that we can mentor girls and give advice and guidance we wish we had received.

What do you think are emerging trends within your industry?

Storytelling was one of the top emerging trends of 2016 within this field and one of the most interesting to track. I've always been so passionate about connecting a brand's story to my story and making sure that along the way my readers are receiving some sort of benefit, whether that is instruction, entertainment, or education. However, in 2015 more and more people dubbed themselves as influencers, and because of the influx of accounts, blogs, and mobile-friendly sites, there had to be a way for influencers to differentiate themselves. Now, when a brand wants an item styled for a blog's audience, they want it to be connected. We are now humanizing monetary items by not just saying that we wore it but by describing why we wore it, how we wore it, and whom we wore it with. It's been exciting to see bloggers that used to only focus on aesthetics in the sense of photography and web design now become writers.

What advice do you have for someone starting out in your industry?

My biggest advice is to find your niche and make it as specific as possible. You can always branch out from your specialty, but it is especially difficult to zone in. In order to beat Google and win search engine optimization (SEO), you have to make your target consumer as small as possible, which is the exact opposite of what your business instincts will tell you. For example, I'm from the South, so my target was originally southern girls. However, that is a market already taken. I then honed in on my Texas background and really style my clothes to fit the market. Almost 3 years later, and my largest audiences are New York, California, and Chicago. These readers like to read something different than

(Continued)

(Continued)

what they see every day, and they were able to find me online because I wasn't competing with a large audience.

What are the three most essential skills for success in your industry?

1. Being a given, creativity is what differentiates you from your competitors and allows brands to want to work with you because they know they are getting a different product. I always make my blog posts extremely personal and have no issue discussing my family, faith, and personal life. Some brands, of course, don't want to work with that, but a lot do because they know that it is humanizing their product.
2. Writing skills are another given, because if you are writing about clothes every single day for years on end, you have to be able to make them relatable in new ways.
3. Lastly, you will go even further if you can make changes on your website through simple coding. Brands require quick turnaround times, so having camera skills, Photoshop skills, and the ability to add in ads and specific margins on your site allow you to meet their needs on timing.

INSIDER INSIGHT

LEE WOLVERTON, MANAGING EDITOR

Describe a day in the life of your job.

My daily duties and routine include, among other things, the following:

- Lead budget meetings in the morning and afternoon to review upcoming stories and determine story play
- Oversee reporting and editing efforts on our top stories
- Discuss story angles and reporting ideas with editors and reporters
- As needed, edit and review stories for merit and legality
- Communicate regularly with editors to ensure we're on top of the day's developments as well as long-range planning and projects

What are the biggest misconceptions about your industry?

The biggest misconception about our field is that of bias, promulgated by people on both sides of the ideological divide, especially those who get a great deal of their information from television networks. There's also a misconception that these are news-gathering operations. In fact, they are not. They are televised talk from people who rely almost entirely on the work of journalists to provide fodder. The work we do is far more difficult than anything many of these talking heads can fathom. Information must be verified. Sources who can and will talk must be found. Reporting and writing must be objective. We are here to inform, not opine.

Another big misconception relates to the state of journalism. Journalism is more alive than ever. Write it down: Journalism isn't going away. It's getting stronger. Digital analytics show us that it works, that people read serious journalism, provided the stories are told well.

What is the best professional advice you have received?

You're only as good as your last paper. That's an old newspaper line that I heard from my first editor 30 years ago. I was feeling pretty good about myself at the time, and he wanted me to know that whatever I'd done was only temporary. You'll have good days and bad days. It can crush your spirit if you let it, but if you believe in what you're doing, you have to get back at it. Each day is a new opportunity to shine or stumble.

What are a few things you wish you had learned in school about your career?

This question makes me think of an old Bruce Springsteen line: "We learned more from a 3-minute record, baby, than we ever learned in school." I learned more in my first day in newspapers than I ever learned in school. No training is better than what I got on the job.

What do you love most about working in your industry?

In our industry, it's a process of constant learning and new experiences every day. That means the job never gets stale. You've never learned it all. You've never reached the peak. You're always climbing; you're always growing. What I love most is the ability to make a difference and the way we accomplish that. All we have are the power of the facts we're able to gather and the might of our storytelling. But when we dig and fight for those facts and we tell good stories about an issue that matters, we can drive change—change that makes a difference, that makes places and circumstances better. That's an absolutely extraordinary thing. It's hard work. It often doesn't pay off in the way that you'd hoped, but when it does, there's no feeling quite like it.

What advice do you have for someone starting out in your industry?

I would advise people to go to a school with a strong newspaper and website program, develop expertise in a particular area—whether it's in political science, the environment, or something else—and study that in school and then work at the school paper or freelance and land a summer internship, rather than studying journalism exclusively. Our field is one in which you learn by doing, not by reading or talking about it. Position yourself to do journalism rather than study it.

(Continued)

(Continued)

What are the three most essential skills for success in your industry?

1. Curiosity is number one—an innate desire to understand how things work, why people do the things they do, to know exactly what happened. The lack of it will leave you missing one story after the next.
2. A healthy cynicism about people, especially people in positions of power and influence and most especially those in positions of public trust, is essential. You cannot be blind to a person's faults or capacity for wrongdoing.
3. Finally, an insatiable drive to get the story, a willingness to keep pushing through obstacles is an absolute must. The real measure in many great stories is the difficulty in getting them. If you aren't determined, you'll be defeated. Tenacity is a prerequisite for any great journalist.

JOURNALISM JOBS: BY THE NUMBERS

Annual median pay in 2016 for reporters and correspondents

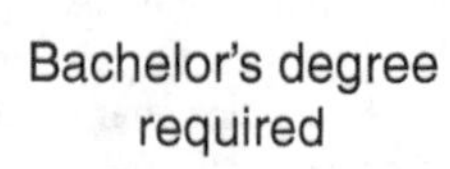

9% decline in available jobs

Ad sales are to blame

Jobs in technical writing are increasing and more lucrative.

Source: Adapted from the U.S. Department of Labor (2016).

SKILLS NEEDED FOR JOURNALISM

The following skills are typically desired for careers in journalism. This is not an exhaustive list.

- Curiosity
- Interviewing
- Media relations
- News value
- Photography
- Production
- Research
- Storytelling
- Writing

JOB SEARCH TERMS

The following is a preliminary list of job search terms that can be used to jump-start your own job search in journalism.

- Broadcast journalism
- Copywriter
- Correspondent
- Editor (assistant, associate, section)
- Freelance writer
- Producer
- Reporting
- Staff writer or news writer

5

MASS COMMUNICATION CAREERS IN BUSINESS

When you're in college, choosing a major can feel like a really huge commitment to one career path. For example, choosing communication as a major might make you feel like your dreams of working in business are over. But careers in mass communication actually have a lot of overlap with careers in business. It's important to remember that every single business relies upon communication for success and needs at least one person to help them communicate internally and externally. Therefore, a background in communication can be extremely valuable to a business career.

WHAT IS BUSINESS?

You may be thinking that this is an obvious question; however, it is important to operate with the same definition of business to determine and understand the role of mass media. A business is an organizational entity involved in providing goods and services to consumers (O'Sullivan & Sheffrin, 2003). Businesses can be privately or publicly owned. Similar to the definition of *mass media* and *mass communication*, the focus is again on the audience, which in business is a consumer, like it is with advertising and marketing. The main goal in business is to make money—otherwise known as a profit, gain, or surplus. Hence, there is the prevalence of the term *return on investment*, or ROI, within other industries—particularly mass communications industries. The ROI is one way that a business can assess the effectiveness of a decision, so being able to show profitable value from communications campaigns is essential. Throughout this book, specific types of businesses will be discussed, including nonprofit and public administration business industries. First, it is important to know the role of mass communication in business so that you can better determine which industry you would like to work within and how you can use your mass communication background most effectively for success.

THE ROLE OF MASS COMMUNICATION IN BUSINESS

No business can function without mass communication. Mass communication efforts are what establish a relationship between a business and a consumer, a market, and society. Mass communication is needed at all levels of business, from inception to closing, and throughout every industry. Therefore, mass communication is going to forever be a relevant field of employment and can withstand market growth and changes in business.

Let's start at the beginning to understand the role of mass communication in business. Imagine you want to start a new business: a luxury campground in your hometown. What do you need to do first? You will need to do a lot of things, but most important, you need to inform the general public of your new business venture. How will you do this? You can engage social media channels, pitch stories to local media outlets, and begin talking with other business owners and potential guests. You cannot start your business without mass communication. You will need to rely on mass communication for publicity throughout the start-up phase. Without publicity, you cannot be competitive within your target market, and without mass media and communication, you will not get publicity. The start-up stage of a business is a prime time to begin working with public relations (PR) and advertising professionals to create a strategic communications plan and start engaging with your target publics.

After you've started your business and received initial publicity, you need to work on carving your home within the market and forecasting demand for your business. This is a great time to conduct market research and gather information about the communications strategies of your competitors. You can then leverage this information to build stronger, more impactful communication campaigns. You will also need to run a website, maintain social media, and manage customer service to run your new business. Each of these roles requires the expertise of a communications professional. Once your business has had time to flourish, you will need to continually assess and adapt your communication strategies to continue to engage consumers and potential opportunities within the marketplace. This will also help you remain competitive.

Mass communication is also needed for general communications relating to business operations. For example, you need mass communication to announce a change in ownership, location, or name. You also need to rely on mass communication to promote sales as well as to inform consumers of sales or product changes. As briefly discussed in the chapter on PR, many organizations engage in corporate social responsibility (CSR) efforts. Mass communication can be used to internally and externally educate audiences on CSR initiatives and increase involvement. Finally, mass communication can help people form public opinions about a business, which can make or break a company. Think for a minute about how the communications of BP negatively affected their business following the *Deepwater Horizon* incident. On the other hand, look at how a business such as TOMS has used mass communication to gain support and awareness.

MASS COMMUNICATION CAREERS IN BUSINESS

As discussed in the chapters about advertising and marketing and PR, these careers are needed in all different types of industries. However, there are some roles that are inherently mass communication jobs specific to business. These potential careers are outlined in what follows, but this is not an exclusive list. Some organizations have additional roles that are best suited to someone with a mass communication background, so be sure to do extensive research when job searching.

Spokesperson

The role of a spokesperson is sometimes a PR role, but it varies among organizations. A company spokesperson is essentially the "face" of an organization and responsible for maintaining the public image for a business and creating and maintaining relationships with relevant partners, other organizations, and consumers. Specifically, when a crisis occurs, the spokesperson is responsible for informing the public. Typical job duties may include writing press releases, conducting media interviews on behalf of the company, and advising on advertising and PR initiatives.

Executive Coach

An executive coach is a consultant that works with top leaders to improve their communication skills. They may train executives to write and give better speeches or interviews or to communicate more effectively with organizational teams to increase business effectiveness. Executive coaches often train executives on media communication strategies such as interviews and public statements.

Recruiter

Recruiters are responsible for bringing new talent to organizations and rely heavily on mass communication channels, like social media, to find job candidates. This type of career is closely aligned with human resources (HR) but use advertising, marketing, and PR strategies and tactics to execute their responsibilities. Megan's Insider Insight provides more information on corporate recruiting.

Brand Representative

Brand representatives work with marketing and sales departments to help increase brand value through representing the brand to consumers. Brand representatives operate in a role similar to a spokesperson but with different objectives. Brand representatives are often tasked with attending trade shows, promoting the organization online, and creating events to build brand awareness (Burks, 2016).

INSIDER INSIGHT

KERI GAVIN, DIRECTOR OF HOST RELATIONS AND CUSTOMIZED TRAINING

Describe a day in the life of your job.

I foster and nurture relationships with communicators at Fortune 500 companies to bring our corporate communication conferences to their organization's headquarters. We tailor the conferences to fit their communicator's needs, so they receive free training for hosting the event.

What are the biggest misconceptions about your industry?

I think people disregard communications as a profession because it's something that we are born to do. However, being an effective communicator is a skill that must be learned and improved upon.

What is the best professional advice you have received?

Always be a student of your work. Have an insatiable curiosity.

What are a few things you wish you had learned in school about your career?

I studied journalism in college. It did not prepare me for the corporate communications world. I wish I would have learned more about the structure and need for communications within global organizations and Fortune 500 companies.

What do you love about working in your industry?

I love the power of delivering a message and seeing how people react. My job as a communicator is to take boring information and make it interesting. I enjoy that challenge.

(Continued)

(Continued)

What do you think are emerging trends within your industry?

Social media continues to take the communications industry by storm. With every new social media platform, communicators need to determine how they can use it to their benefit.

What advice do you have for someone starting out in your industry?

Be a sponge. Absorb everything you can. You can (and should) learn something from everyone.

What are the three most essential skills for success in your industry?

1. To be an effective communicator, you need to be confident in what you're saying. Being clear and concise is equally important.
2. You have to be able to change what you're doing at a moment's notice. The need to get important information out to people will always call for last-minute changes.
3. Being an effective communicator requires a human and authentic side. I think that is a must in your interactions with colleagues (to get the necessary information from them) and in your writing.

How has networking influenced your professional life?

Networking is my job. Without it, I would not be successful. I think of every stranger as a friend I haven't met, and I try to find commonality with everyone I meet.

How do you suggest someone stay up to date on your industry and remain competitive?

Keep up with industry news, find new connections in your industry, attend conferences, and engage in personal development opportunities.

INSIDER INSIGHT

MEGAN SOMMER, CORPORATE RECRUITER

What is your job description?

Currently, I work for a global hearing technology company. I work specifically for one of the specialty hearing aid brands out of their corporate headquarters. This is a high-profile role where I am responsible for the acquisition and hiring of new talent for corporate as well as our individual business locations throughout the country. I work in conjunction with department hiring managers to proactively source, screen, and procure new hires into various critical roles. I also support the human resources (HR) department and management teams in a variety of HR functions including, but not limited to, recruitment, onboarding, data entry, and other administrative duties. I need to be a proactive member of the HR team, who constantly seeks to improve workflow and best recruitment practices. I also take point on a variety of HR projects that are specifically related to recruitment and talent acquisition for North America.

Describe a day in the life of your job.

My day to day can change depending on which project I need to work on. I am currently involved in rebranding and updating the careers page on our corporate company website. Every day I have to work inside of our applicant tracking system in order to open jobs, post to career websites, and screen résumés.

I am on e-mail all day working with outside vendors like LinkedIn or Indeed.com and working with business owners and hiring managers on their day-to-day hiring needs. Every week includes various phone and in-person interviews in order to pass candidates on to the next step of the hiring process.

What are the biggest misconceptions about your industry?

I think there is often confusion around the differences between being an "agency headhunter" or a "corporate recruiter." There are many types of recruiters, but working internally as a corporate recruiter means that you work for one company as their employee and hire for that organization only. You are like an ambassador for the company. Headhunters typically work for multiple companies. Candidates will often seek career coaching or advice from their recruiter, and as a corporate recruiter, you cannot provide that feedback because your loyalty is to the company and not to the candidate.

How have mentors influenced your career?

Mentors were always around me during my education and early on in my career, but until I began my current role, I didn't realize the relationship could be beneficial in helping me grow my confidence. The past few years I have had someone who has had a great career in my current industry be a great coach to me and unselfishly push me to reach my goals. He gives great high-level and detailed advice to me and has helped me conquer my fears of speaking in front of large crowds.

What are a few things you wish you learned in school about your career?

I never knew being a corporate recruiter was even a career option when I was in school. I never realized it was something I could use a communication degree toward.

(Continued)

(Continued)

What do you love about working in your industry?

Interviewing and placing people into their jobs has been a rewarding career. When someone genuinely attributes your help with them finding their passion in their career, it is a wonderful feeling.

You also get to have unique and personal conversations with people every day and contribute to building an organization from the inside out. I look around at the people I work with and realize they are here because of my efforts. That is exciting.

What do you think are emerging trends within your industry?

Social media mediums like Facebook and Twitter are quickly becoming very popular resources for hiring and getting the word out about internal job openings. The faster you can have a candidate apply to a position from a mobile device, the more applicants your organization will have. Finding out if they are the right fit for the role will happen later on in the process. Making it convenient for someone to apply to a job is most important these days.

What advice do you have for someone starting out in your industry?

I think getting some longevity with one company or recruitment agency early on in your career is important. You want to show that you can be stable, and if possible, try to go for a promotion within your first two years. If promotion opportunities are not available, then look for the next step in your career.

What are the three most essential skills for success in your industry?

1. Networking ability
2. Relationship building
3. Positive attitude

How has networking influenced your professional life?

Keeping in touch with other professionals is the key to success as a recruiter. I cannot be afraid to talk to everyone and connect with people because you never know who might lead to future opportunities.

How do you suggest someone stay up to date on your industry and remain competitive?

Every day I spend time on LinkedIn and other sites to learn about emerging trends. I am truly interested in talent acquisition, so that makes me want to learn more about where the industry is going.

I like to be able to educate my organization on what is working for our competitors and other companies. I have been able to conduct this research and educate my employer on new technologies that we have implemented into our day-to-day recruitment processes.

MASS COMMUNICATION CAREERS IN BUSINESS: BY THE NUMBERS

$47,696

Average salary for recruiters

$61,980

Average salary for spokesperson

Bachelor's degree required

21% increase in available jobs over next 10 years

There are over 1 million people employed in mass communications roles in business.

Sources: Adapted from PayScale (2017) and Suttle (n.d.).

SKILLS NEEDED FOR MASS COMMUNICATION

The following skills are typically desired for careers in mass communication. This is not an exhaustive list.

- Business knowledge
- High energy or outgoing
- Interpersonal communication
- Networking

- Organization
- Public speaking
- Research
- Social media
- Teamwork
- Writing

JOB SEARCH TERMS

The following is a preliminary list of job search terms that can be used to jump-start your own job search in mass communication.

- Brand representative or ambassador
- Business communications
- Corporate communications
- Executive coach
- Recruiter
- Spokesperson

PUBLISHING

Publishing is a robust industry that can be a great fit for entry-level jobs and lifelong careers for people with educational backgrounds in mass communication. People who are passionate about reading and love getting lost in a good story but have studied public relations (PR) or marketing would be well-suited to a career promoting new books. If you find yourself constantly correcting grammar and editing your friend's text messages and social media posts, you might make a great editor. However, as the Insider Insight profiles indicate, working in publishing can be demanding and stressful, but it does not come without great reward to those who are committed to the industry.

WHAT IS PUBLISHING?

Publishing is the dissemination of information for sale. *Merriam-Webster* defines *publishing* (2017) as "the business or profession of the commercial production and issuance of literature, information, musical scores or sometimes recordings, or art." Publishers make information available to the public through forms such as literature or music. People typically think of publishing as a book-related industry, but technological advances have expanded the field tremendously. Today, publishing exists because of three inventions: (1) writing, (2) paper, and (3) printing. However, it is the social development, the importance and spread of literacy, which has made publishing a lucrative industry (Tucker, Unwin, & Unwin, 2015).

HISTORY

The history of publishing is really a culmination of other inventions that have collectively evolved into a booming industry. The advent of the printing press by Gutenberg allowed for the first book to be published in 1440. Publishing became an enterprise since the cost to print a book was lowered and distribution was increased. Book printing and distribution continued throughout Europe, but it was not until 1640 when the first book was published in the United States (Orcutt, 1930). *Bay Psalm Book* was printed in Cambridge, Massachusetts, used for over a century, and went through many editions (Orcutt, 1930). Then, in 1690, the first U.S. newspaper was published (for more information, see Chapter 4). The first magazine followed the new publishing trend and was published in 1741 by Andrew Bradford and Benjamin Franklin (Magazines.com, 2016). Three days later, Benjamin Franklin independently published *General Magazine.* Unfortunately, neither was met with great success, and within 6 months, publication had ceased (Magazines.com, 2016). However, by the end of the 18th century, there were more than 100 magazines in circulation throughout the United States (Magazines.com, 2016). Following the printing press, the typewriter and then computers continued to advance publishing for both writers and publishers alike.

TODAY'S TRENDS

Today, traditional publishing is still a lucrative industry, but publishing has expanded to online platforms. Digital publishing is also referred to as electronic publishing (or e-publishing) or online publishing. It includes the digital publication of books, magazines, and newspapers and distributes them through online channels that include websites, tablets, and mobile applications. While some people may argue that print is dying, that does not mean that publishing is also dying. Due to digital publishing, the industry continues to grow and expand, which provides a lot of opportunity for careers. If you have an interest in using multiple online platforms, the skills needed to reach niche audiences, and the desire to work in publishing, digital publishing may be the perfect fit.

Self-publishing is another emerging trend. Self-publishing is the publication of any material without the involvement of a publisher. Some authors find self-publishing beneficial because they remain in complete control throughout the writing, editing, and publishing process. However, they must rely on printers to print their material, and some self-publishing authors seek help with design, marketing, and distribution. Therefore, self-publishing provides some opportunities for potential careers but not as many as traditional publishing. In 2008, there were more self-published books than those published traditionally, and within 1 year, over 75% of all books released were self-published (Milliot, 2010).

CAREERS IN PUBLISHING

Although many entry-level job candidates set out to simply get a job in the publishing industry, tailoring your skill set to the different areas within publishing can arguably make you a better employee. Publishing consists of several different areas—each one necessary to create and sustain a publication. Like systems theory would argue, each component of the industry is important, and they are all interdependent. It can be inferred, then, that starting out within one area of publishing does not prohibit you from moving into another area later in your career. The subindustries of publishing will be outlined within this chapter, beginning with editorial careers. However, an important precursor to searching for a job in publishing is deciding whether you want to work in trade or academic publishing.

Trade publishing includes the books and magazines you tend to read for fun, like literary fiction, some nonfiction, travel- and food-related periodicals, and so on. Due to the popularity of trade publications, it can be a difficult area to break into. Trade publishing is also very commercial where you must have a sharp eye for sales and mass adoption potential. Finding success for trade clients and authors moves beyond exceptional writing; it requires strategy and a hands-on approach to produce a best seller. Working in trade publishing provides the opportunity to work closely with authors to improve their ideas and their writing. It also requires a business-savvy mind-set, as contract negotiations and promotions are vital within trade publishing (O'Connor, 2014). What is one perk to working in trade? You get a lot of advance copies of books, so if you are an avid reader, this might be the right track for you.

Academic publishing produces the books you typically use during school and cite in papers and research. Academic publishing works to craft insightful material and original research. As opposed to working with authors in trade publishing, academic publishing affords you the chance to work with professors around the world in an effort to bring their research to specific audiences to spark intellectual dialogue. This area of publishing does not include the same pressure as trade publishing to make something a best seller or craft ideas for mainstream success. Here, the ideas take precedence over potential sales. If you are a person who enjoys research and considers yourself a lifelong learner, then academic publishing might be a great home for your career. Careers in academic publishing are also well suited to people who are considering graduate school or looking for an intellectual alternative to graduate school (O'Connor, 2014).

Editorial

This is arguably the most commonly recognized area in publishing. Aiming to begin your career in publishing as an editor, though, is likely unrealistic. Instead, starting out as an editorial assistant can help you climb the ladder toward an editor position. Editorial assistants are on the front lines for publishing organizations. Editorial positions are the heart of the publishing industry. They are responsible for meticulous record keeping, mediation, and author relations. In essence, you are an assistant to your editor and the author alike, trying to keep both parties happy and on schedule. This role is similar to the account coordinator or manager positions described in the chapters about marketing and advertising. As you advance, you can expect greater interaction with authors and a more critical role in the pitching and negotiation phases of projects (O'Connor, 2014).

If you were to review job postings for editors, here are some of the descriptions you might find. Editors prepare, rewrite, and edit copy to improve readability or supervise others who do this work. They also read copy and proofread for grammar, syntax, and appropriate formatting and publication style. Allocating space for content is another important role that editors often complete in tandem with art directors and designers. Finally, editors also develop, plan, and pitch content ideas before overseeing the production of that content for publication.

Production

How many times have you been in a bookstore or online and looked at something simply because it visually caught your attention? This is the value of production—well, one value at least. Production editors are responsible for ensuring that manuscripts are edited, designed, proofread, and printed. This career brings information to life and helps to give it meaning in the marketplace through visual design. Production editors and assistants also work closely with authors to help determine a style and brand for the publication. Production editors assist with the layout and design of the text as well as the formatting and style of the publication. Production is a lot of behind-the-scenes work that ties everything together. This career is well suited to creative, critical thinkers and problem solvers who can manage multiple projects and tight deadlines as well as work harmoniously with other departments (O'Connor, 2014).

Marketing, Promotion, and Publicity

At this stage, the publication is forthcoming, so you need to let people know. If you find yourself liking PR or marketing but also have a strong passion toward a career in publishing, look no further than publishing promotion. Think about a book jacket for a moment. Usually on the back or inside, you see short, quoted reviews by well-known and respected names. These are thanks to the marketing and promotions team of the publisher. When you see authors on television shows, quoted or written about in periodicals, this is also the work of a promotional publishing team. In a nutshell, working in this subindustry in publishing requires you to build excitement and demand around publications. It requires persistence, no fear of rejection, and great tenacity. It can also be highly rewarding when you know that you are part of the reason for a publication's success.

Sales

Jen, featured in one of the Insider Insight profiles in this chapter, works in advertising sales for a journal publication. This is one potential career domain. Sales keep publishing houses and organizations going. It is what allows editors and authors the continuous opportunity to work together. Without sales, publishing fails. Remember, the business of being in business is to make money. Publishing sales roles can be in-house positions (e.g., for publishing houses), self-sufficient commission roles, or agency jobs where you work with numerous publishers. Similar to marketing and promotions, a sales representative has the same goal: to build excitement over forthcoming publications. However, they have a different motive: to sell the publication to bookstores, other sellers, and consumers. This career requires great sociability and a passion for reading and sharing knowledge. It can also require substantial traveling. As one sales rep explains, "Selling means making an impact on the people who, in turn, impact your average reader just by shelving a book in their store. I put the books out there—I can give the little guys a chance. And I think that's pretty amazing" (Di Gregorio, 2012).

CAREER DOMAINS

Now that you have a better understanding of the types of careers available within publishing, it is important to narrow your search to the right type of publication. There are various publications, as will be outlined, so read carefully and conduct your own independent research to choose the best fit. This list is not mutually exclusive but can help you begin your exploration into publishing careers.

Newspapers

Approximately one-third of publishers in the United States are newspaper publishers (U.S. Department of Labor, 2016). Therefore, this is an area of publishing that is ripe with opportunities for recent college graduates. Newspapers generate revenue not only from sales and subscriptions but also from advertising. This provides sales and advertising careers as well as marketing opportunities. Due to the segmented nature of newspapers—meaning they write on a variety of topics—there is a lot of writing and editorial work. Freelance opportunities are a great way to break into the newspaper industry if you're having trouble securing a full-time position. Newspapers rely on multiple editors, production and design assistants, and writers to put together regular content—often on tight schedules and deadlines. More information about careers with newspapers can also be found in Chapter 4.

Magazines and Journals

Magazines and periodicals are another area for careers in publishing. These are publications that appear with new content on a regular schedule, similar to newspapers but often with less frequency. Not including newspapers, periodical publishing also makes up about one-third of the U.S. market (Matsa & Mitchell, 2013). However, magazine publishing has been declining in recent years. It is estimated that in 2013, subscription levels for 22 of the top 25 magazines declined, and only 3 gained subscribers (Matsa & Mitchell, 2013). Although new online magazines are popping up, and some traditional magazines are embracing online publishing schedules. Academic and trade journals are not experiencing the same dips in subscribers but are integrating their content to online platforms. For example, some academic journals allow to you subscribe solely online and download articles from their websites rather than receive a hard copy for each new issue.

Books

Book publishing is what most people tend to think of when they consider careers in publishing. Similar to newspaper and periodical publishing, careers in book publishing require marketing, promotions, and sales. However, book publishing also requires a lot of negotiation and contract knowledge. There is also the need to determine how the book will be distributed, which often requires strategic planning and decision-making. On-demand printing and delivery of books is continuing to increase in popularity, and electronic textbooks are also gaining in popularity. Determining how to distribute a book on the front-end influences the design and promotional costs and strategies to maximize success. Although many publishing houses exist, 60% of books produced in the United States come from one of the Big Five publishing houses: (1) Penguin Random House, (2) Hachette, (3) HarperCollins, (4) Simon & Schuster, and (5) Macmillan (Losowsky, 2013).

INSIDER INSIGHT

PADDY CALISTRO, PRESIDENT AND CEO

What is your job description?

As co-owner of an independent publishing company for the past 25 years, my job has no specific description. I oversee everything in the company except the financials, but my copublisher by necessity keeps me informed about the numbers, so we can both proceed with decisions in a fiscally responsible manner. I oversee all hiring and firing. I negotiate with printers. I work with authors and graphic designers, proofreaders, public relations (PR) people. I supervise publicity and marketing. There is no facet of the business that I am not familiar with.

Describe a day in the life of your job.

- 3:30 a.m.—Read e-mails from international contacts, including printers to solve any problems that may exist before I start the day in California.
- 6:00 a.m.—Check e-mails that may come in from the East Coast.
- 9:00 a.m.—Start the day at my desk, addressing other e-mails and phone calls that have come in.

- 10:00 a.m.–12:30 p.m.—Have meetings with authors and potential authors and printers.
- 1:00 p.m.–6:00 p.m.—Have editing time: line editing, proofreading, talking to authors about their text, reviewing proofs, and reviewing designs.
- 6:00 p.m.–7:30 p.m.—Meet with copublisher to discuss financials and the business side of publishing.

What are the biggest misconceptions about your industry?

- That it is glamorous to be a publisher
- That because you read a lot, you will make a good editor
- That good books sell and bad books don't
- That some writers don't need editors
- That books are dead

What is the best professional advice you have received?

- Make sure to pay your printer on time.
- Trust your own judgment.
- Don't work with an author you don't like.

What are a few things you wish you had learned in school about your career?

I would have liked to know more about the nuts and bolts of getting books printed so that I didn't have to learn that by the seat of my pants. There are aspects of book manufacturing that are fascinating and aspects that are totally boring, but understanding the full process is essential for a publisher, especially as times and technology changes.

What do you love about working in your industry?

I love the fact that each book I edit is like a master's degree in the topic. Some of those topics would have never been offered to me in college. Each new book is a step into a part of my world that I have not explored before. I love that.

What advice do you have for someone starting out in your industry?

- Stay current by reading newspapers and blogs as well as listening to chatter around you.

(Continued)

(Continued)

- Be truly interested in people who talk to you; don't dismiss ideas because they differ from your own.
- Be as open to being edited as you expect your authors to be.
- Always listen to the ideas of people who are at least 5 years younger than you are, and as you age, square that number—or at least be mindful of the fact that younger people know a lot of things that you don't. Value those ideas, and try to see how what's new fits into what you produce each day.

What are the three most essential skills for success in your industry?

1. A sense of what's new and interesting before other people think it's new and interesting
2. The ability to question a statement that is presented as fact if you have any doubt whatsoever
3. The openness to look beyond what you've done before and try something new

INSIDER INSIGHT

MOIRA KERRIGAN, ASSOCIATE DIRECTOR OF MARKETING

Describe a day in the life of your job.

My day ranges from the big stuff to the little things—everything from strategic thinking about how we are going to market and promote a new book to inviting booksellers to join us for events. There are always tons of meetings—catching up on the latest from the sales team's most recent meetings, getting updates from the publicity team on media hits and author tours, calling authors to discuss the marketing plans for their books, and grabbing coffee with sales reps from some of the trade publications we work with regularly.

What are the biggest misconceptions about your industry?

I think there is a misconception that marketing is all about the strategic thinking but doesn't involve a lot of nitty-gritty execution. This couldn't be further from the truth. Once you've gotten a partner on board to work together on a promotion, there is so much granular work that needs to happen from requesting creative to communicating with authors getting approval from legal and a lot more.

Most ideas start as something grand, but in order for any campaigns to actually be built and to succeed, there are a lot of legwork things that need to get done.

What is the best professional advice you have received?

Fill your workspace with your achievements. For me, this manifests itself in a desk littered with the latest and greatest projects I've worked on—from tote bags I've helped produce for trade shows to my most successful bookseller letters and everything in between. This is an everyday reminder to myself and everyone who stops by my desk about the great work we're doing.

How have mentors influenced your career?

The best mentors I've had have been people who trust me to figure things out and get my job done on my own. Feeling like I have the support and room to think creatively, generate new ideas, and work at my own pace (sometimes fast and sometimes slow) has been such a gift for me in my career.

What are a few things you wish you learned in school about your career?

I never studied marketing, but I wish I had taken more classes on marketing and more business classes in general. It has been fascinating learning how to utilize analytics to determine return on investment (ROI) and engagement. I wish I had learned more about that in school before starting my career.

What do you love about working in publishing?

I love book publishing. It is the industry I have wanted to work in my entire life. The whole process of taking a book from the seedling of an idea into a finished product out in the world with the potential to affect change in the life of hundreds of thousands of people will never cease to excite me. In particular, I love that working in book marketing allows me to work with so many people and departments, both within the company and outside of it—from the art, production, and editorial departments, to booksellers across the country, to business media contacts, and other third parties. And, of course, the authors. It's so much fun to get to peek into the worlds of so many interesting, smart, and creative people.

What do you think are emerging trends within your industry?

It has always been true that book publishers have long been looking for the next big thing: The idea is to publish a book at just the right moment when there is a fever pitch of interest around a subject matter, particular author, etc. A focus in recent years has been to publish the book of authors who have a large platform online, whether it be Instagram followers, YouTube celebrities, and the like.

(Continued)

(Continued)

I think that is starting to lessen a bit as publishers realize that just the virtue of having a lot of social media followers isn't enough to sell an entire book.

What advice do you have for someone starting out in your industry?

Be as voracious a consumer of the world you can be. This doesn't necessarily mean buying lots of things, but what it means is paying attention when you're out in the world to what is happening. For publishing, that means you should be paying attention in bookstores, yes, but also in the gift market, in the media, in your day-to-day interactions with products you pick up in the grocery store, podcasts you listen to, the topics of conversation your friends keep bringing up. On the surface, this is easy to do. It simply means to continue to pursue the things you are interested in and consider them in a new context. In general, I think the most important thing in any work environment is forging relationships with the people you work with as well as other people in your industry. It's amazing how much time and effort just knowing the right person to ask about something can save you.

What are the three most essential skills for success in your industry?

1. In order to be a good marketer, you must be an effective communicator. This goes for communicating with everyone from authors, to designers, to partners. You must be able to work with everyone from the publisher and president of a company to the person in the mailroom.
2. You must be able to work on both long and short timelines. A book can take 1 year, or 2, or 10 to finally make it to the printer. You have to be able to be just as excited about working on a project for a long time as you are for projects you are churning out.
3. And, finally, you have to love the product you're working with. You may not want to take home a copy of every single book you work on, but you do need to be able to find the value in each book and the need each book meets.

How do you suggest someone stay up to date on your industry and remain competitive?

You must pay attention to industry news. What's happening on the large scale with the publishing industry as a whole, but also what's happening on a more granular level? What are the books that are resonating with people? What are the bookstores doing to bring people into their stores? What's happening with the algorithms on Amazon? There are a number of newsletters I subscribe to in order to stay current—Shelf Awareness, Publisher's Weekly, Publisher's Lunch, Beth Golay's Books & Whatnot, Literary Hub, and the newsletters of competitive publishers.

INSIDER INSIGHT

JEN BRADY, ADVERTISING ASSOCIATE

What is your job description?

I coordinate the writing and editing for all advertisements for a well-known medical journal. I work with both digital and print advertisers who are publishing career opportunities and real estate ads.

Describe a day in the life of your job.

My job requires a lot of customer service and computer skills. I take phone calls, e-mails, and faxes from advertisers and answer a lot of questions about how to submit their ads. I also have to explain pricing a lot. Our journal is published biweekly, so there are always deadlines to be met. Once everything is in for each issue, I work with another person to edit each ad to fit our style guide. I also have to check that our online ads are published when they are supposed to be and fit within their own guidelines.

What are the biggest misconceptions about your industry?

That advertising is free. Some advertisers think that you don't have to put a lot of thought into the wording of your ad and then complain when they don't get any replies. We also have people who think they should get refunds if no one replies to their ad.

What is the best professional advice you have received?

A former boss told me it's always easier to apply for work when the people interviewing you have already heard of you. I've taken that to mean you should work on your own projects outside of work. It shows you're passionate, and it's great for networking. I know one of the reasons I got hired is because I had experience volunteering as an editor and blogger. Find blogs or nonprofits you like, and e-mail them to see if they can use your help as a volunteer editor, e-mail creator, writer, etc. I can't stress volunteering enough; it also keeps you feeling fulfilled and purposeful.

What are the three most essential skills for success in your industry?

1. Being kind to everyone: your boss, your clients, your coworkers.
2. Learning new technology, such as hypertext markup language (HTML), search engine optimization (SEO), and Photoshop. You're more marketable when you have more computer skills.

(Continued)

(Continued)

3. Being empathetic. Always think from the customer's point of view when writing an ad. Read it and have other people read it, and ask yourself if you (as the customer) would want what you're selling.

How do you suggest someone stay up to date on your industry and remain competitive?

Find some online personalities that do what you want to do professionally. Subscribe to their newsletters, follow them on social media, check out their LinkedIn profiles. If they are the type to constantly update and share trends, this is an easy way to stay informed.

PUBLISHING JOBS: BY THE NUMBERS

$57,210 2016 median average pay for editors

Bachelor's degree required

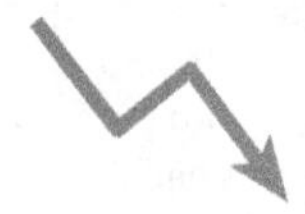

In 2014, there were 117,200 jobs for editors, but that's expected to decline by 5% over the next 10 years.

Technical writers made an annual median salary of $69,850 per year in 2016, and the job outlook for technical writers is expected to increase by 10% over the next decade.

As of May 2017, there were approximately 723,500 people employed in the United States by the publishing industry. In 2016, there were roughly 35,000 people working in publishing sales and marketing, 50,000 editors, and 18,000 graphic designers in publishing.

Source: Adapted from the U.S. Department of Labor (2016).

SKILLS NEEDED FOR PUBLISHING

In addition to the skills described throughout the chapter, Publishing Trends (2011) outlines additional skills needed to succeed in a publishing career. The following list was generated from industry insiders and a content analysis of currently available publishing positions.

- Creativity
- Curiosity
- Data analysis and evaluation
- Flexibility
- Grammar and writing
- Marketing knowledge
- Multitasking
- Networking
- Online communication
- Organization
- Reputation management
- Sales

JOB SEARCH TERMS

The following is a preliminary list of job search terms that can be used to jump-start your own job search in publishing.

- Account manager
- Acquisitions editor
- Assistant editor
- Content editor
- Content publisher
- Digital publishing
- Junior publishing associate
- Marketing coordinator
- Print production

TELECOMMUNICATIONS AND VISUAL COMMUNICATION

When you go on a family vacation or spend a great weekend with friends, do you take a million photos and then rush home to put them into a video highlight reel? Katie, featured in one of the Insider Insight profiles in this chapter, does, and that was her first signal that a career in visual communication would be the right fit for her. But maybe you're obsessed with the radio or dying to be an on-air personality or announcer? If so, telecommunications is an industry made for you! If not, but you love the idea of working in a newsroom or radio station, there are still many fruitful opportunities for you in telecommunications.

WHAT IS TELECOMMUNICATIONS?

Telecommunications is the transmission of signs, signals, messages, and sounds by wire, radio, optical, or other electromagnetic system (International Telecommunications Union, 2012). More simply, telecommunications is the exchange of information through the use of technology. Telecommunications is often abbreviated and referred to as "TCOMM." This is also sometimes referred to as mediated communication. Telecommunications cannot exist without media, including but not limited to the Internet, television, and mobile phones. It is because of telecommunications that we can communicate faster and with broader audiences, even globally. As we continue to adopt new technologies, the field of telecommunications will evolve accordingly.

Although we characterize telecommunications today as communication using technology, the first instance of telecommunications was absent of any technology. In fact, it was the pigeon that used to help distribute messages and is credited with early examples of telecommunications. Pigeons were used by the Greeks to carry the names of Olympic victors to other cities and were also used to fly stock prices to other places (Reuters, 2008). When the telegraph was invented, the use of carrier pigeons ceased. The first transatlantic telegraph was completed in 1866 (Dibner, 1959), demonstrating how technology has increased our ability to expand our communications, even from an early start. A decade later, the telephone was invented and further altered our ability to communicate with others, including at faster and less expensive rates. However, the telephone was originally marketed as a business tool and a way to order services, not as an interpersonal relationship maintenance tool, as we use it today.

With the invention of the radio, followed by television, the telecommunications industry continued to expand. Suddenly, people were able to receive news even faster, for longer durations, and shared between broader audiences. Radio, as we still experience today, also allowed for two-way telecommunication between organizations and people. Television, of course, evolved to become a way to not only disseminate information but also promote products and events, and until the overtaking of the Internet and social media, it was primarily used for one-way communication transmission. The Internet is another example of telecommunications. Data are shared through technology online to users and uploaded by users to the Internet. This demonstrates how the Internet can allow for both one- and two-way communications. While the primary evolution of telecommunications has been for business purposes, telecommunications has undoubtedly changed our social landscape. Advances like text messaging and social media websites are two of the most prominent examples.

CAREERS IN TELECOMMUNICATIONS

You are likely already familiar with many of the career opportunities available within telecommunications but may not have realized they would be categorized in this industry. In what follows is a brief overview of some career options a person studying telecommunications could pursue postgraduation. Potential careers include broadcast journalism, video production, and radio production.

Broadcasting or Announcing

Careers in broadcasting can range in opportunities. For example, news reporters, correspondents, and analysts typically have some telecommunications education if not a major in telecommunications. These professionals inform the public about news and events on local, national, and international levels. This is a profession available for those interested in television, radio, or more print journalism. This can be a very competitive field, requiring a substantial amount of time "in the field" hunting stories and leads often on tight deadlines. The median annual wage for reporters, correspondents, and broadcast news analysts was $37,720 in 2012 (U.S. Department of Labor, 2015). Unfortunately, this industry is expected to decline by approximately 9% between today and 2024 (U.S. Department of Labor, 2015).

Another avenue within broadcast journalism is the role of an announcer. Announcers are used for communicating sports information as well as introduce, moderate, and conclude events. Announcers also get tasked with making special appearances and commenting on relevant news. While reporting and news anchoring are full-time careers, announcers can work either full- or part-time. In 2012, the median annual wage for radio and television announcers was $28,020. The lowest 10% earned less than $17,270, and the highest 10% earned upward of seventy thousand dollars per year (U.S. Department of Labor, 2015).

If you are interested in broadcasting but would prefer to be behind the camera, a career such as a station programmer or program director is a better fit. Station programmers are responsible for determining the content that will best capture the target audience. Program directors are responsible for creating the "feel" of a station and work closely with managers, marketers, and salespeople (Wetfeet, 2012). The program director plans, schedules, and evaluates programming. This requires a lot of strategic planning and data management.

Another career behind the camera is that of a producer. Producers are responsible for the seamless entertainment we enjoy regularly. They must integrate a station's content and coordinate the scheduling of programming with the right mix of news, entertainment, education, and advertising. Producers also manage the workloads of the announcers, anchors, reporters, writers, and other producers. Often referred to as a director, producers oversee the production of shows and commercials, while also putting everything together in a way that makes sense to the viewers. The median salary for TV producers in 2015 was $68,440, and the U.S. Bureau of Labor Statistics predicts a 9% faster than average growth in producer jobs by 2024 (U.S. Department of Labor, 2015). There is also robust marketing for video production, which can be done for independent firms and agencies or in-house for organizations and/or communication networks.

Finally, telecommunications and broadcasting cannot survive without audiovisual (AV) technicians and writers. The technical aspects of broadcasting include setting up, operating, and maintaining electrical equipment for television broadcasts. This career has an annual salary of $41,780 as of May 2015 (U.S. Department of Labor, 2015). Writers help create the content we consume. News writers write the news reports read on-air by announcers, anchors, and reporters. Copywriters are utilized to help produce content for commercials, and scriptwriters write the material used in original entertainment programming including comedies and dramas. The salaries for writers vary substantially, and often, writers work on freelance opportunities or for multiple organizations simultaneously.

Radio

Radio is similar to television, but also has inherent differences. Thus, the career possibilities in radio overlap to those offered in broadcasting but also have other more specific roles. Typically, a president or general manager manages radio stations. The general manager oversees the budget, sets annual and long-range objectives, and manages the various departments. They also ensure the station is complying with Federal Communications Commission regulations and disseminate all station policies to employees. The role of a radio station general manager is not suitable for a recent college graduate, but it is an aspirational career. Those with an interest in radio but do not have the required on-air skills or experience to be a general manager can assume a role with various departments including accounting, marketing and advertising, or administration.

Similar to broadcasting, radio also requires a programming director. Programming directors typically report to the operations director and often are responsible for programming across multiple radio stations. Program directors help create promotions that promote the content of the station, and when a station does not have a music director, the program director also handles the music programming. The music director helps determine which songs get airtime and which do not. However, many radio stations in larger markets have automated their music libraries and do not require a full-time music director (Chuday, 2008). The average salary for a programming director in radio is approximately $43,000.

As you well know, radio stations flourish based not only on the music they play but because of their on-air talent. Often referred to as DJs, cohosts, or radio personalities, this career requires a great personality and the ability to be conversational and knowledgeable on a broad range of topics. Radio DJs play and mix music and discuss topics in between songs. On-air personalities, however, are not responsible for actually playing and mixing music. Instead, on-air personalities spend a lot of time conducting "show prep," where they research trends, hot topics, and news stories to share engaging and relevant content with radio listeners. DJs are typically required to stick to a station playlist predetermined by either the station's programming or music director. Full-time DJs tend to be salaried employees, while on-air personalities can either be salaried or paid hourly (Careers in Music, 2015).

Just like careers in broadcasting, radio requires sound technicians and audio engineers. Additionally, radio provides career opportunities for those interested in sales, marketing, advertising, and public relations (PR). Radio stations rely on promotions to boost their listeners and remain relevant. Sales, advertising, marketing, and PR departments must be able to work seamlessly with program directors, DJs, and on-air personalities to help reach the overall goals for the station. Lastly, radio requires producers who help work the soundboard, generate show ideas, and identify program guests (Chuday, 2008). Some stations also employ assistant producers; the assistant producer position is typically entry level for those starting out in radio.

INSIDER INSIGHT

DUTCH WARGO, CAMERAMAN

What is your job description?

I am a cameraman for Fox News Channel. I am based out of Chicago but get sent out on local and national assignments as needed. I have covered major sports events, political events, protests, and newsworthy trials. I am responsible for shooting real-time footage of events that is used by Fox to put together news stories.

Describe a day in the life of your job.

No day is ever the same. I shoot and edit news stories pertaining to current events. One day I could be following Trump on the campaign trail and the next covering the World Series. My job is unpredictable, and I am often on call, so my hours can vary as well.

What are the biggest misconceptions about your industry?

People think I just point the camera and hit a record button, but there is more to it than that. I try to visualize a story before I shoot it. I also collaborate with the reporters and producers to determine the focus of each story so I know what sound and video to obtain.

What is the best professional advice you have received?

Keep a positive attitude.

How have mentors influenced your career?

Mentors have influenced me tremendously. Once I decided this was the field I wanted to be in, finding the correct mentor helped guide me along my career journey.

What are a few things you wish you had learned in school about your career?

That it doesn't pay very well, even if you're working for a big market or station.

What do you love about working in your industry?

I do something different every day. I get to travel the United States and cover current events. I am often present when records are broken and history is made—for good or bad reasons.

What do you think are emerging trends within your industry?

Using camera phones and social media to deliver news more quickly.

What advice do you have for someone starting out in your industry?

Make sure it's what you want to do, and then commit to it. Don't do it half-assed.

What are the three most essential skills for success in your industry?

1. You have to listen to what people say to effectively communicate your story.
2. You have to be able to talk to anybody from top-level CEOs, politicians, and everyday people.
3. Keeping a positive attitude is everything, especially when news isn't always fun or positive.

How do you suggest someone stay up to date on your industry and remain competitive?

Watch the news. Watch national and local news. Watch documentaries. Try to gather new ideas on ways to shoot and tell stories.

SKILLS NEEDED FOR TELECOMMUNICATIONS

The skills needed for specific jobs will vary. However, generally, in order to obtain an entry-level position postgraduation in telecommunications, the following skills are necessary. This is not an exhaustive list. Skills were gathered from content analysis of current job descriptions and advertisements as well as from the U.S. Department of Labor (2015). Undoubtedly, in this industry more than others, relevant experience through internships and hands-on learning is the key skill sought by employers. Any previous experience should be compiled into a portfolio to demonstrate the specialized and technical skills so many telecommunications careers require. In what follows are general skills desired for success in any aspect of telecommunications and then skills relevant to both broadcasting and radio are outlined.

- Ability to manage stress
- Attention to detail
- Data analysis
- Flexibility
- Oral communication
- Written communication

Broadcasting

- AV knowledge
- Camera knowledge
- Content development
- Film editing
- News writing
- On-air presence
- Reporting experience

Radio

- Audio editing
- Industry experience
- Live talk experience
- Music knowledge
- Production
- Radio writing
- Sound engineering

JOB SEARCH TERMS

The following is a preliminary list of job search terms that can be used to jump-start your own job search in telecommunications.

- Account manager
- Analyst
- Assistant or associate producer
- Entry-level broadcasting
- Entry-level radio
- News copywriter
- On-air announcer (radio/TV)
- Production assistant
- Project manager
- Radio promotions
- Technician
- Telecommunications

WHAT IS VISUAL COMMUNICATION?

Visual communication is the transmission of information and ideas using symbols and imagery. It is considered one of the three main types of communication along with verbal and nonverbal. Visual communication is arguably the type of communication that people rely on most because it includes signs, graphic designs, films, and typography, just to name a few. You may have learned about visual communication in school under a different name: semiotics. Semiotics is the study of how people make meaning out of symbols and how symbols are interpreted.

Cave paintings are most likely the beginning of visual communication. But as societies advanced and more people began to travel, the need to communicate effectively despite language barriers led to the implementation of pictograms. Pictograms are images that represent physical objects and were used to share information or ask questions. For example, someone could show a pictogram of a money sign and a loaf of bread to ask where he or she could go to buy bread. Visual communication continued to evolve with technology like the printing press, newspapers, and books, as discussed in other chapters. However, the invention of lithography in 1798 allowed for art reproduction. Then, propaganda efforts relied heavily on visual communication for persuasion throughout the early 1900s. Today, the Internet and digital printing provide faster access to information, interactivity, and personalized information. This is an industry that is overtaken with trying to satisfy people's visual needs.

Trends of visual communication today include large, high-quality images to capture and maintain our attention. However, people also like semiflat designs. Semiflat designs are fast and easy to process but are still visually appealing in part due to their simplicity. The use of semiflat designs is commonly seen in infographics. In 2012, the *New York Times* published "Snowfall," which told the story of an avalanche using large photos and videos to elicit emotional responses from readers (Branch, 2012). This began the trend of content experiences that create emotional, visual experiences through content. Today, storytelling has become more intimate and visual (Newbold, 2016).

CAREERS IN VISUAL COMMUNICATION

The most commonly associated career with visual communication is that of a web or graphic designer. Graphic designers create visual concepts, either using computer software or by hand, to communicate ideas that inspire, inform, and captivate audiences (U.S. Department of Labor, 2015). Graphic designers help develop the overall layout and production design for websites, advertisements, brochures, magazines, and corporate communications. Graphic and web designers are utilized in almost every aspect of mass communication, including, but not limited to, publishing, advertising, marketing, PR, nonprofits, public administration, and telecommunications. Many graphic and web designers supplement their full-time work with freelance work or volunteer work to continue to build their personal portfolios. However, the average annual wage for graphic designers in 2015 was $46,900 (U.S. Department of Labor, 2015). Graphic designers need to have a background in communication to understand the effect and reach of their messages, but graphic designers also need to have training in art. A background in computer programming such as hypertext markup language (HTML) and cascading style sheets (CSS) can also be essential to a successful career in graphic design. One benefit of graphic design is that it offers many opportunities to do freelance work, which can be invaluable during the early years of a career.

Graphic designers are also expected to have a robust portfolio showcasing their work, and this can include work done throughout your collegiate career.

Another popular career for visual communicators is that of an art director, at the assistant, associate, or senior level depending on experience. Art directors are responsible for the visual style and images in magazines, newspapers, product packaging, and movie and TV productions. They create the overall design of a project and direct others who develop artwork and layouts. Art directors oversee the work of other designers and artists who produce images for a variety of mediums, which requires great teamwork and patience. As of 2014, about 15% of art directors work for advertising and PR firms, while others worked for newspaper and magazine publishers (U.S. Department of Labor, 2015). About half of all art directors reported being self-employed as of 2014 (U.S. Department of Labor, 2015).

INSIDER INSIGHT

KATIE DOLCIATO, ASSOCIATE ART DIRECTOR

What is your job description?

I am an associate art director for *Cleveland Magazine*'s custom publishing department. I work on multiple magazines for various different clients including city and city chambers, nonprofits, local businesses, and more. I design layouts, with either assigned or freelance photography, or supplied art. I am also responsible for branding for select clients including maintaining websites, logo design, and more.

Describe a day in the life of your job.

Depending on where we are in the production of the magazine, the days are different. In the custom department, we are assigned three to five magazines a month. The magazine is set in stages before print. (These are the stages that we follow as a company, which may be different for every publishing company.)

- Stage 1: The client meeting occurs about 3 months before the magazine is printed.
- Stage 2: Prep begins about 2 weeks before printing when content for the stories starts to come in from the writers. The designers will look over the stories and decide if photography should be collected from the sources or if we should hire a photographer to take photos.
- Stage 3: Photography can include a photo shoot that the designer can choose to attend at their discretion.
- Stage 4: The designing of the layout begins with advertisements and edit ratios. The design process lasts for about 2 to 5 days depending on the size of the magazine.

- Stage 5: Proofing and changes occur based on the client's review and feedback.
- Stage 6: Production will commence. Any color corrections on photos will be made, and the magazine will be prepared for the printer. The production manager will send the files to the printer.

What are the biggest misconceptions about your industry?

With graphic design, I would say the biggest is that our work is easy. A lot of people find graphic design to be more of a hobby than a job, but it is more about problem-solving and, more importantly, conveying a message.

What is the best professional advice you have received?

"Don't take your job home." It is easy to get consumed by your job, but it's more important to separate work from home and try to keep a work–life balance.

What are a few things you wish you had learned in school about your career?

I wish I would have learned more about the different levels of experience within my field and the different salaries associated with each one.

What do you love about working in your industry?

Change. Every client and every piece that you work on is different. The industry is always coming up with new trends, and every client wants something different. Each day is different, and each design has its own unique twist to it. I enjoy working in the publishing industry because I am able to reach an audience and send a message. My job, in a nutshell, is to get the reader to read the page that he or she is on. Making a design interesting enough to keep someone on the page is a challenge that I enjoy about the field.

What advice do you have for someone starting out in your industry?

Intern. See which area of graphic design is right for you before you graduate. Intern at as many places as you can, and try to get credit through co-op programs.

What are the three most essential skills for success in your industry?

1. Listening skills are essential because you will either have a client or an editor giving instructions on what they want your design to look like.

(Continued)

(Continued)

2. Creative skills are important because you will need to come up with different ideas for everything you create. No two magazines or logos can look exactly alike, and each story and client deserves a different treatment to the design.
3. Organizational skills are also critical to design work because you need to keep everything straight. Design is a field driven by hierarchies, so whether keeping the organization of one design or the organization of three different projects that you are working on at one time is critical.

How do you suggest someone stay up to date on your industry and remain competitive?

Finding inspiration in things will keep you up to date. The best designers are the ones who can take a story and find the meaning behind it and be able to show an audience that it is worth reading.

SKILLS NEEDED FOR VISUAL COMMUNICATION

The following skills are typically desired for careers in visual communication. This is not an exhaustive list. This list was compiled from the U.S. Department of Labor (2015) and a content analysis of current job postings.

Adobe Creative Cloud
Creativity
Detail-oriented
Flexibility
Graphic design
Organized
Photography
Print media
Social media
Teamwork
Web design
Written and oral communication

JOB SEARCH TERMS

The following is a preliminary list of job search terms that can be used to jump-start your own job search in visual communication.

Assistant or associate art director
Graphic designer
Visual communication associate
Visual designer
Web designer

TELECOMMUNICATIONS AND VISUAL COMMUNICATION JOBS: BY THE NUMBERS

$47,640

Median annual salary in 2016 for graphic designers

$65,300

Median annual salary in 2016 for multimedia artists and animators

$34,070

Median annual salary in 2016 for photographers

$89,820

Median annual salary in 2016 for art directors

$70,950

Median annual salary in 2016 for producers

$30,830

Median annual salary in 2016 for announcers

Most jobs in telecommunications require a bachelor's degree.

The telecommunications industry is expected to remain and grow at a stable rate for the next decade.

As of 2017, there were over 700,000 U.S. residents working in telecommunications.

Source: Adapted from the U.S. Department of Labor (2015).

8

PUBLIC ADMINISTRATION

If you're reading this book from cover to cover, then until this point, the discussions of careers has been pretty specific. You've read about working in agencies, television and radio stations, production, publishing, and other unique environments and industries. Public administration, however, blends all of those things but also has its own niche. Careers in public administration encourage people to serve in nonprofits, public and private sector, and the government. While many specific skills are needed for careers in public administration, the field cannot exist without strong communicators. If you enjoy public service while also crafting and delivering messages to various audiences, read on to learn more about public administration.

WHAT IS PUBLIC ADMINISTRATION?

Public administrators are public servants working in public departments and agencies at all levels of government, including city, county, regional, state, and federal departments (Kettl & Fessler, 2009). The field of public administration is multidisciplinary and composed of six subfields: (1) human resources (HR), (2) organizational theory, (3) policy analysis, (4) statistics, (5) budgeting, and (6) ethics. Careers in public administration can provide opportunities to be city managers, HR administrators, budget directors, and cabinet secretaries. Since public administration is the translation of politics into the daily reality for citizens, mass communication is vital.

Public administration is the implementation of government policy (Perry & Christensen, 2015). It is concerned with the organization of government policies and programs as well as the behavior of officials (usually nonelected) formally responsible for their conduct. Public administration has also been defined as the management of public programs (Denhardt & Denhardt, 2015). Public administration dates back to the early 18th century in the form of pages, treasurers, and tax collectors for kings and emperors. During this time, public administrators were considered the eyes and ears of rulers, often due to their abilities to read and write, setting them apart from other commoners. Even during this time, much like today, the roles and responsibilities of civil servants were vital to government entities. In the United States, Woodrow Wilson is considered the father of public administration from his article *The Study of Administration* in 1887. Within this article, Wilson outlined four concepts central to public administration: (1) separating politics and administration, (2) conducting comparative analysis of political and private organizations, (3) improving efficiency with businesslike practices and attitudes, and (4) improving the effectiveness of public service through management and training civil servants. Wilson's concepts led other scholars to advance their own ideas about public administration, and in 1939, the American Society for Public Administration (ASPA) was formed. Today, the ASPA (2016) is the largest and most prominent professional association within the field of public administration. Throughout the next three decades, until about 1970, public administration surged due in large part to the success of the United States. However, it was also during this time that public administration faced a lot of scrutiny due to Vietnam and Watergate. Following World War II, public administration evolved to include policymaking and analysis, which remains a part of the industry today.

CAREERS IN PUBLIC ADMINISTRATION

Before discussing the myriad of career options available to someone who wishes to pursue public administration, here is a note about educational credentials. Given the multidisciplinary nature of the industry, undergraduate curriculums typically do not fully prepare someone to enter the field of public administration and thrive. Therefore, many master's degree in public administration (MPA) programs are offered. Should you wish to pursue a lifelong career in public administration, obtaining an MPA may be required at some point. This is not to discredit, however, the importance of entry-level experience in public administration. In fact, many employers offer tuition reimbursement programs and may be proactive in helping you get your MPA.

Careers in public administration are part of public sector organizations. The public sector is the part of our governmental system that provides services. Hence, the term *public servant* is used to describe individuals working in public administration. It includes the military, police, infrastructure (roads, lighting, water supply), public transportation and education, and elected officials. Organizations that are not a part of the public sector are part of the private sector. Private sector businesses aim to earn a profit and are not under direct control by the government (Wigmore, 2013). The public sector should also not be confused with the voluntary or nonprofit sector, which will be discussed in Chapter 9.

One of the most robust areas for careers in public administration is in government. Elected and appointed officials at the local, state, or national level are public administrators. These positions include the mainstream and more visible positions like governor, senator, secretary of state, and representatives. However, there are a lot of other elected careers available, including school board members, county commissioners, county auditors, county treasurers, county prosecutors, court clerks, city managers, aldermen, and town council members. Each one of these positions requires different skills and levels of experience, but a brief overview of each is warranted.

School Board Member

This is an elected position, typically with a 2-year paid term. To be an eligible candidate, you must reside in the school district and be capable of voting on school-related issues.

County Commissioner

This is typically a full-time, 4-year paid position to serve on a board with at least three others. Any resident of the county can vote in this election. The board acts as the executive of the local government and administers county governmental services, including road maintenance, public health issues, and property registration.

County Auditor

Depending on the county, this may or may not be an elected position. If it is not elected, it is appointed. It typically has a full-time, 4-year term and is held by someone with accounting and auditing experience, although anyone is eligible to run. The county auditor oversees all of the financial books for the county and administers the budget.

County Treasurer

This is an elected, full-time, 4-year position. County treasurers are responsible for sending tax bills, receiving funds, and collecting overdue payments. The treasurer then distributes that money among various government agencies.

County Prosecutor

This is typically a high-profile, elected position. The term is normally full-time for 4 years. However, you must be an attorney to be eligible to run. The county prosecutor acts as the chief legal officer for a county and works in tandem with others. They are responsible for prosecuting felony cases.

Court Clerk

City clerks are elected to a full-time, 4-year term. Although a law degree is not required, most clerks are attorneys. The county clerk files vital records relating to births, deaths, and marriages. This role is one of the oldest known officials of local government.

City Manager

Depending on the city, this can be either an elected or appointed position. City managers typically have experience with urban planning. They are the chief liaisons between the city's elected officials and the citizens. They must issue reports to the public about policies, budgets, and other public information.

Alderman

This is a great entry-level career opportunity because although it is an elected official, it is a part-time, 2-year term. Aldermen campaign only in their own ward, making their base of voters smaller. They serve on the city council board and act as advocates for the ward citizens.

Town Council Member

Town councils are legislative bodies of townships made up of elected trustees. The trustees perform duties similar to those of a city council member. This is a part-time, 2-year term.

As you can see, there are many different options available for a career in public administration, so this is not an exhaustive list. As a public administrator, you have the responsibility of using communication to engage with multiple audiences, sometimes simultaneously. You need to communicate with internal audiences, like fellow employees, but you also have various external audiences you need to inform. External audiences might include community members, other officials, families, children, elderly, and community organizations. Working in public administration gives you the unique opportunity to touch a broad audience through your communication tactics. As you well know, how ideas and information are communicated can make all the difference between the success of a program and the failure, so as a public administrator, you must have strong and strategic communication skills. Those with specialized public relations (PR) or marketing skills can also find a home in public administration—perhaps working for a city or village on issues of tourism or helping to advocate and promote certain issues and legislation. Public administration professionals must also remain in good standing with journalists to help obtain and, when necessary, control media coverage. Mass communication plays an important role in public administration because of the different stakeholders involved. This requires strategic communication practices and thoughtful execution and evaluation of campaigns.

INSIDER INSIGHT

JIM NORRIS, VILLAGE MANAGER

What is your job description?

As village manager, I am the chief administrative officer of the Village of Hoffman Estates, hired by the village president and the board of trustees (elected officials) to run the daily operations of our municipal government. Hoffman Estates is a community of 52,000 people in northwest suburban Chicago with a budget of $110,000,000 and 365 employees. I am responsible for all aspects of the daily operation, including budget and finance, personnel, hiring, firing and discipline, and implementation of policy and programs in departments through the hiring and management of the following department heads: police, fire, public works, information, systems, human resources (HR), health and human services, development services, finance and general government.

Describe a day in the life of your job.

This is the wonderful part of my career; no day is exactly like another. One day I could be working and negotiating with a developer on locating a corporate headquarters in our community, and the next day I could be hearing an employee or union grievance. I meet with residents, businesses, community groups on issues, and concerns and opportunities. I am involved in governmental groups related to centralized public safety dispatching, solid waste, Lake Michigan water, and other things.

What are the biggest misconceptions about your industry?

I think the biggest misconception about the field of city management is that we are in our positions because we knew somebody or because we are political hacks. That is patently not true in this profession where most go to school to receive a master's degree in public administration (MPA) and then matriculate through a career starting as a management analyst and ultimately work through advancement or through changing communities to be department heads, deputy managers, or city or village managers.

How have mentors influenced your career?

Mentors are extraordinarily important in this career. Listening and learning from their successes and failures as well as having a sounding board when big issues occur is a wonderful opportunity. One of the things I am most proud of over my 35 years in the profession is the role I have been able to play in mentoring and teaching young professionals.

What are a few things you wish you had learned in school about your career?

I wish I had learned how to balance work–home obligations and responsibilities. That was something I had to learn on my own.

What do you love about working in your industry?

I love the fact that every day is different and that we have the ability to positively impact the quality of life of individuals and communities.

What do you think are emerging trends within your industry?

Emerging trends are being more focused on effectiveness rather than just efficiency and economy along with increasing use of networks and collaboration.

What advice do you have for someone starting out in your industry?

Realize that this is the public sector and that transparency is reality. Listen effectively.

What are the three most essential skills for success in your industry?

1. Communication, even in a world of technology, is still the most important skill. Being able to write effectively and communicate verbally is huge.
2. The next is listening and truly hearing what is being said.
3. Last is to be intimate with your budget. A successful manager will know the finances of the community inside and out.

What professional groups do you belong to, and how do those influence your career?

International City/County Management Association (ICMA), Illinois City/County Management Association (ILCMA), Metropolitan Managers Association. They influence my career in a variety of ways. The ICMA has promulgated a code of ethics that is extremely important in this profession. ICMA and ILCMA publish newsletters and professional resources as well as hold training sessions and annual conferences. Continuing education in this field is very important.

(Continued)

(Continued)

How do you suggest someone stay up to date on your industry and remain competitive?

Go to annual conferences and ongoing training to receive continuing education and to learn about best practices. Network with professional colleagues both formally and informally. While I do all of these things personally, I also teach at the graduate level as an adjunct instructor, and I find that by keeping current with material through teaching, my knowledge level is reinforced on a regular basis.

INSIDER INSIGHT

MICHAEL CROTTY, ASSISTANT VILLAGE MANAGER/ DIRECTOR OF HUMAN RESOURCES

What is your job description?

I am the assistant village manager/director of human resources (HR) for the Village of Wheeling. This is a professional position with primary responsibilities providing senior manager support to the village manager in all areas as assigned to ensure effective accomplishments of village objectives and for administration of the village's HR system and labor relations system. I am responsible for personnel management, coordination of various interdepartmental matters, and assistance with special research and reports. My work includes managing the village's HR system, programs, policies, labor relations, contract administration and benefits administration, program evaluation, budgeting, and general policy administration. Specifically, my responsibilities include personnel recruitment and selection, wage and benefit administration, contract negotiation and administration, employee orientation and coordination of training, disciplinary and workplace investigation, policy development, communicating goals, objectives, and programs to village departments and the general public. In the absence of the village manager, I act in his or her place.

Describe a day in the life of your job.

A typical day is difficult to describe because the role of the assistant village manager is that of a professional generalist. In my case, I also hold the position of director of HR, so it is not atypical that I would be reviewing personnel policies against changes in state and federal law and making sure the organization is consistent with those new laws and changes. When workplace issues or complaints are raised, it falls to my office to investigate or cause them to be investigated, depending on the type of complaint and severity. When the municipality's labor contracts near their expiration dates, I ensure that management is prepared for those negotiations by researching contracts in other communities, analyzing wages and benefits, meeting with departmental managers to identify issues, strategizing management's approach for branding, etc. After that preparation, I am the chief labor negotiator for management and lead the negotiations for management for police, fire, and public works contracts. One of the softer skills that the assistant village manager position calls for is to listen to issues brought by department heads and other employees and, where appropriate, provide advice on how to handle those issues. Some of this can be categorized as coaching or even as gatekeeping for issues to the village manager. This position provides oversight to a number of functions handled by a full-time HR coordinator, particularly benefits administration and recruitment. There is a fair degree of coordination answering questions and brainstorming with that position to make sure the municipality is keeping up with Affordable Care Act requirements, health plan design changes, advertising, and filing vacancies as they arise. During budget season, the position joins the village manager and finance director to meet with all departments to review budget requests in order for the village manager to ultimately present a budget to the elected body for its approval.

What are the biggest misconceptions about your industry?

One of the biggest misconceptions is the understanding that local government public administration is a field at all—and particularly that there is a professional city manager position charged with carrying out the policies and administration of the municipal corporation. There are various forms of local government, and I work in what's called council-manager form. When I have told people in the past that I am an assistant village manager, a very common response is "Oh, so you're like the mayor?" In fact, there are municipalities that are strong mayor forms, and in those places, the mayor is, in essence, the CEO. However, the vast majority of municipalities are council-manager forms, and in those places, the mayor and elected officials are not staff. Instead, the elected board hires a professional city (or village) manager charged with running the operations of the village and carrying out the policy as set by the elected board. This is a very important distinction, as the village manager and staff are considered merit-based personnel. The result of public administration consists of professionals trained in their various disciplines (e.g. finance, public works, urban management, planning) who serve the community through professional service rather than politics.

What is the best professional advice you have received?

Don't make it up. Avoid the trap that you need to have all the answers in real time. Buying yourself time to come up with an acceptable, appropriate, and correct

(Continued)

(Continued)

answer is not only a good idea but results in far more professional credibility than giving a quick answer that doesn't turn out to be right.

How have mentors influenced your career?

I have had three primary mentors—(1) a professor in graduate school, (2) one of my first supervisors in the profession, and (3) a village manager who had worked both in the public and private sector. If I were to focus in on how each one of these mentors has influenced my career, it would be that, in different ways, they each bolstered my confidence in my abilities. With respect to the graduate school professor, she had a style that welcomed all comments and interactions in the classroom. She was quick to laugh at jokes made during class (which I was known to do a lot), yet was an expert at taking every comment and question and squeezing the value out of them for the benefit of learning. She made it possible and comfortable for all of us to have a voice even in the early stages of our careers. My first supervisor put me, as an intern, in front of the elected body for the first time and had me present a full recommendation on a project for which I was the lead. He told me just before I was to get up there not to be nervous and just "tell them what you know." Twenty-three years later, I still remember those calming words every time I am called upon to present. Finally, and most significantly, I worked for 6.5 years for a village manager who I consider to be one of the brightest, no-nonsense, and supportive individuals I have ever met. He often would publicly credit me for my instincts, and specifically, when he saw an aptitude in me for labor relations and collective bargaining, he stood back and let me lead those functions. As a result, I have specialized in labor relations and currently hold a national board position with the National Public Employer Labor Relations Association. He believed that a successful mentee was a reflection of him as well, and of all, he truly made me realize that I had something to offer this field.

What are a few things you wish you learned in school about your career?

There is a lot of talk these days about millennials in the workplace. One of the qualities that is often attributed to this group is finding work that makes them feel like they are making a difference. I appreciate the generational categorization, but I don't know if that characteristic is unique to millennials. Many of my friends and I started our careers in public administration years ago, at least in part, for the same reason. That said, many of the municipal services that the public receive from the people committed to this profession almost necessarily require that those public administrators be taken for granted. Water comes out of the faucet when you turn it on, garbage gets picked up, road and capital projects get funded, the street lights work, etc. I often tell people that one of the measures of success for doing my job is that the public can take me for granted on a daily basis. I'm good with that, but that perspective would have been a good one to have back when I was new entrant to the field. The nuance that should not be lost is that you can still be making a difference even if you don't always hear the roaring crowd.

What do you love about working in your industry?

I can think of no other industry where the work is more varied than in public administration and, particularly, city management. In the nearly 25 years that I have been in this field, I have been involved in, responsible for, and/or provided oversight to budgeting, finance, public improvements, construction, public safety, HR, collective bargaining, risk management, parks and recreation, emergency management planning, social and senior services, library services, and so on. In addition, there is the whole art and discipline of being responsible to the public in ways that the private sector is not. We often hear in our profession that government needs to run like a business. There is some truth in that, and I think over the years there have been lessons from the private sector that have made it into the public sector. However, it is very important to remember that representative democracy and its extension into public service introduces an element that is not always found in private business. Efficiency can serve to be at odds with representativeness. For example, it could be argued that running a senior center serving a small number of members in the community is not the most efficient use of tax dollars. However, it is not unusual that such service is determined to be a core function by the elected representatives of the community and, as such, a viable and necessary expenditure of funds. The nature of the work and the way that work impacts the public is a driving force.

What do you think are emerging trends within your industry?

Particularly since the great recession of 2008, local government has been trying to answer the call for consolidation and partnership in responsible ways. This stems from doing more with less, since most municipal organizations cut staff significantly during that period. This trend is only going to continue. We are seeing more creation of joint emergency dispatch centers, calls for equipment and personnel sharing between municipal borders, insurance cooperatives, and more. There is also a move toward regionalization of public safety (particularly fire departments). Second—and this is one that I have noticed growing over time—I believe that American society and its politics are becoming more and more populist, and this is changing the way that city managers look at their jobs and the profession. There is a much greater call and expectation for transparency in government. Watchdog groups, residents, and the press all want greater access to information. It is difficult to find a municipal website these days that doesn't have a parking space labeled *transparency* on which you can find reports, budgets, labor contracts, salaries of employees, minutes, and so forth. I believe this is a function of our real-time media society as well, but it is a significant trend nonetheless.

(Continued)

(Continued)

What advice do you have for someone starting out in your industry?

Take your opportunities. If it scares you, dive in and do it. Experiential learning is at least as equally important as academic learning. I was fortunate to attend graduate school in a geographic location where there is an abundance of local government bodies. As such, the academic program was bolstered by the available year-round internships doing real work, working on real projects, and being exposed to the real nuts and bolts of municipal management. As an intern or a new professional, be eager for new projects and trust that you will be able to work through those things on which you have no experience. Also, public administration is a career that plays out in a fishbowl. Everyone is watching. Be respectful, be kind, and focus on being an ethical and good person. It sounds cliché, but these three things have carried me farther in my profession than anything I learned in a book.

What are the three most essential skills for success in your industry?

1. Empathy and openness builds trust that you can understand different viewpoints and that you will make decisions based on reasonableness.
2. Stay focused on the big picture. Public administrators often find themselves challenged by competing viewpoints, whether from elected officials, staff, or the public. It is easy to get distracted and be drawn down rabbit holes. It is essential to remember what the end goal is and to base decisions with that goal in mind.
3. Develop yourself. Most jobs require this, but public administrators can never stop developing themselves professionally if they intend to be successful. Trends change, laws change, the culture of the workplace changes, and all of these things mean that we need to change.

How do you suggest someone stay up to date on your industry and remain competitive?

Aside from the obvious answers like reading, taking advantage of professional development, joining and participating in associations, and networking, I believe it is important to find ways to make yourself useful at every turn. If you want to be competitive, you need to have something to show off. That may be a series of traits and characteristics that you've worked on. It may be a body of knowledge that you've accumulated. The only way to remain competitive is to continue to challenge yourself to grow professionally and learn new things. Finally, try and find something that distinguishes you from others, and make sure you show that.

PUBLIC ADMINISTRATION JOBS: BY THE NUMBERS

Average salary for people working at a managerial level in public administration

Entry-level careers require a bachelor's degree, and senior roles can require a master's in public administration.

Jobs in public administration are expected to increase by 14% over the next decade.

States with the highest employment in public administration are as follows:

1. California
2. Texas
3. New York
4. Illinois
5. Massachusetts

SKILLS NEEDED FOR PUBLIC ADMINISTRATION

In what follows are a handful of relevant skills often overlooked but deeply desirable for a career in public administration. This list was compiled through a content analysis of current job openings at various levels of public administration.

Ability to withhold confidential information

Ability to work with others

Collaborative

Forward-thinking

Organized

Passionate to create or advocate for change

Political acumen

Strong ethics and morals

Strong written, verbal, and nonverbal communication skills

JOB SEARCH TERMS

The following is a preliminary list of job search terms that can be used to jump-start your own job search in public administration.

- Administration
- Civil service
- Community management
- Development
- Municipal service
- Operations
- Program analyst
- Public administration

NONPROFITS

If you were suddenly gifted a large amount of money, how would you spend it? Many people would consider buying material items, but there are also many people who would consider donating it to a worthy cause. The latter are the people who may be well-suited to working in nonprofits. Careers in nonprofits offer the same opportunities as other industries including public relations (PR), marketing and advertising, visual communication, and lots of writing. But careers in nonprofits thrive because of their dedicated employees who choose to work in nonprofits because of their desire to help people, places, and things.

WHAT ARE NONPROFITS?

A nonprofit organization (NPO) is an organization with the purpose of doing something other than making a profit—hence, the literal name *nonprofit.* NPOs are often dedicated to furthering a cause or advocating for a particular point of view. A very mainstream example of a nonprofit you are likely familiar with is the Susan G. Komen foundation for breast cancer research. It is a nonprofit because the money raised funds events, research, and outreach initiatives. It is estimated that nonprofits, along with nongovernmental organizations, are the fastest-growing types of organizations in the world (Hall, 1994). However, what constitutes an NPO is very diverse in scope.

NPOs are tax exempt for two primary reasons: (1) charitable giving and (2) civic organizations. We typically associate NPOs with charitable giving, but other entities such as universities, fraternal organizations, and political parties are also considered NPOs because they are tax exempt. Many NPOs operate using what is called the double bottom line, which explains that the primary objective is to raise money to further the specific cause, but the organization will also use part of the money raised to ensure the organization's sustainability (Grobman, 2008). For example, 75% of money raised might go toward research, events, and outreach, while the remaining 25% is used to pay employees as well as office space and supplies. A board of directors often manages NPOs, since designations as a nonprofit means that there are no owners. Some boards are membership based, while others are elected. NPOs are governed by a set of bylaws, and boards make decisions accordingly.

It is estimated that over 90% of all NPOs currently in existence have been since 1950 (Hall, 1994). The history of nonprofits is tied to politics in many significant ways. Charitable nonprofits, which also rely upon the work of volunteers, saw surges in volunteerism after every war, specifically after WWII and the Vietnam War (Parks, 2009). Political NPOs became more mainstream following the defeat of Barry Goldwater in 1964. It was then that conservative leaders realized they could not win without creating their own "establishments" of think tanks, advocates, and foundations. Reagan then assumed office due in large part to the help and support of NPOs (Hall, 1994). His platform partially aimed to undo the damage of big government stifling private initiatives through a combination of jawboning higher levels of corporate giving and cutting government spending (Hall, 1994). Unfortunately, by the time he took office, nearly one-third of the annual revenue of private research universities came from government spending, and he was unaware just how dependent the nonprofit sector had become on the government (Hall, 1994). Although the political roots of NPOs are documented, the history of charitable NPOs is much more unknown. Nonetheless, trends in globalization and society continue to move the industry of NPOs forward.

CAREERS IN NONPROFITS

There are many career options for someone who wants to work in the nonprofit sector. First, you should establish which type of organization you want to work for, since the field is so diverse. Potential options include advocacy and political groups, professional associations, educational organizations, health organizations, foundations, and environmental organizations. There are also direct social service agencies, health, and religious organizations, too. If it seems too overwhelming to decide what type of organization is the best fit, you can similarly start by deciding what you really care about. Try asking yourself if there is a specific population or issue you really want to work with. Some examples include children and families, disability issues, literacy, homelessness, water quality, senior citizens, prison reform, and consumer rights. Typically, nonprofit employees are motivated intrinsically based on the cause they are supporting. Hence, this is why it can be so competitive to get hired in a nonprofit role. The job retention rates for employees are higher because of the deep commitment employees share with the organization.

Once you have settled upon the type of organization or issue you want to work with, you can move on to identifying the right type of job for you. Nonprofit opportunities fall into three primary categories: (1) direct service, (2) management/administration, and (3) research. However, it is important to understand that

NPOs often require their employees to be "jacks-or-jills-of-all-trades" because although your formal job requirements might be fund-raising, you can also still be tasked with website updates, administrative tasks, speaking engagements, and PR tactics. Nonprofit employees should be ready and willing to assist in all ways and understand that they do not work in silos, regardless of their formal job description.

Direct service opportunities include responsibilities such as community organizing, educating, and counseling in addition to doing social work. Typically, direct service roles require specialized training that someone studying mass communication may not have upon graduating college. However, a background in mass communication can make you very well suited to pursuing management or administration career opportunities in nonprofits.

Management and administration careers are much more aligned with a background in mass communication. For example, a PR coordinator or relationship manager would be considered management or administration roles. Management and administration careers in nonprofit also comprise the program coordinators, marketing and PR practitioners, fund-raisers, human resources (HR), finance, and IT services. As you can see, the management or administration functions within nonprofits are far-reaching but well suited to mass communications. As any seasoned nonprofit professional will tell you, working with NPOs requires great flexibility and teamwork. It is not uncommon that a program coordinator occasionally does graphic design–related tasks or that someone in marketing helps out with fund-raising. The success of NPOs relies on collaboration both within and outside of the organization. Thus, the management and administration roles are vital to the industry. Based on previous chapters, you should have a firm understanding of how marketing and PR operates within a variety of industries, and that is no different for NPOs. Therefore, in what follows is a brief overview of program coordinator responsibilities, the role of HR, and fund-raising and development careers.

Program Coordinator

Program directors are responsible for overseeing the coordination and administration of all aspects of an ongoing program including planning, organizing, staffing, leading, and controlling program activities. The challenge is that multiple programs run simultaneously, so this can sometimes be a time-consuming and stressful job. Program directors plan the delivery of the program in accordance with the mission and goals of the organization. They also help develop and implement new initiatives to support the organization, annual operating plans, long-term goals, and proposal funding. They also have the responsibility to ensure that programs operate in line with all organizational procedures, as well as any state or federal policies. Staffing the program requires picking the best leaders for the right roles to increase the overall effectiveness. Nonprofit programs are not conducted in a vacuum; they require teamwork and systematic collaboration. The program is controlled through reporting, communication with funders and relevant groups, accurate budgeting, and detailed documentation (HR Council, 2016).

Human Resources

Staffing nonprofits is one of the most important decisions. Nonprofits have to address these primary personnel issues: assessing personnel needs, recruiting, screening, selecting and hiring, holding new employee orientation, and dealing with compensation issues (Inc., 2016). The assessment requires HR professionals to fill necessary positions, provide accurate and realistic job descriptions in writing, and provide performance evaluations to help boost performance. Of course, the recruitment is where mass communication plays a key role. NPOs must publicize their opportunities to the right audiences by using the most effective channels. Nonprofits typically rely on local media and community organizations for recruitment (Inc., 2016). The screening and selection process includes interviewing to assess for best fit after carefully reviewing applications. Once a hiring decision is made, the new employee must be properly oriented to their new organization and their new role. This is a very important task that arguably can set people up for success or failure in their role. HR must clearly educate and outline all job expectations to newcomers. Finally, HR employees in nonprofits, just like in for-profit organizations, have to communicate about compensation. This can include tangible benefits like insurance, competitive pay, and professional development; it also includes intangible benefits like the satisfaction of service.

Fund-Raising and Development

The roles of fund-raising and development are vital to the success and sustainability of an NPO. In this sense, development is defined as how NPOs supplement their earned income with donations, grants, sponsorships, and gifts in kind (Idealist, 2016). This is opposed to using the term *development* to describe the scope of work done by an organization. Gifts to NPOs from individuals, corporations, and foundations in the United States total about $300 billion per year (Giving USA Foundation, 2016). Individuals make up approximately three-quarters of that total. Therefore, fund-raising for nonprofits is essential. There are several ways to raise funds, including through obtaining grants, hosting events, and approaching people who can give major gifts. Some NPOs also offer memberships and annual appeals, or yearly requests for donations. Capital campaigns, telemarketing, canvasing, and other fund-raisers like car washes or bake sales are other ways to raise funds (Idealist, 2016). The role of someone working in a fund-raising or development career is to constantly recruit, retain, and manage relationships with potential donors and other organizations. This job requires a constant hustle and a passion for the organization coupled with great sales abilities.

If a role in direct service or management or administration is not right for you, there is one other area of nonprofit work: research. Research roles in nonprofits include policy analysis, quantitative and qualitative expertise, program evaluation, and/or scientific research. In a research position, you may be asked to synthesize high-level research findings to a general audience to help make the case for additional funds. Or, you may be asked to evaluate the success of different programs to help influence long-term planning. Quantitative and qualitative research can be used to inform internal and external publics and to help maintain relationships with different target groups for increased success over time.

INSIDER INSIGHT

EMILY ANDERLY, FUND-RAISING DIRECTOR

What is your job description?

I work for a large nationwide nonprofit organization (NPO), specifically with their youth programs, so I oversee the K–12 educational programs between two states. My goal is to increase awareness of health and wellness, bring resources into schools and families that don't have them, and increase the requirements of physical education in elementary schools.

Describe a day in the life of your job.

The best thing about working for a nonprofit, in my experience, is that no two days are the same. My days vary widely, which is part of the reason I love my job so much. The days also vary based on the time of year, as the winter and spring are so busy for us. But typically, I'm out in the field, meeting with physical educators and superintendents; doing kick-off assemblies; meeting with local for-profit companies who want to sponsor our organization or one of our events; and participating in lobbying efforts in the state capital fighting for tobacco laws, physical education requirements, and a host of other issues. There are days when I go to 12 or 15 schools at a time, all over the state, and there are days when I get to spend the whole day at a schoolwide health event, which is amazing because then I get to interact with the kids and hear the stories and amazing impact that health knowledge and information can have on a young person and their family. It's those days, despite the long hours and extensive travel, that keep me going.

What are the biggest misconceptions about your industry?

I think first and foremost, it's a huge misconception that if you're going to work in nonprofit you can say goodbye to the potential of a good salary. If you're working

(Continued)

(Continued)

for a statewide or nationwide nonprofit, chances are you'll be paid very fairly, and these organizations love to promote from within, so you can find yourself managing a small team and with a great salary within a couple of years. Also, I think there is this perception that it's all work and no reward. Nonprofit work is some of the most exhausting, tiresome, and difficult work out there, but it is also so rewarding.

What is the best professional advice you have received?

To align the nonprofit you work for as closely as possible to what you are most passionate about, because the long days are much easier to swallow if you're out talking about something you truly believe in. There is nothing better than that!

How have mentors influenced your career?

I've had some very impactful mentors over the years, starting with a few college professors that really shaped the way I viewed my future. I think I got so tied up in what I *thought* my career should be and lost sight of what I truly wanted to do. So it took me a few jobs and several years to build up the guts to quit a steady job in finance and take the risk to move to nonprofit, and it was the best decision I've ever made. When I finally sat down and got honest with myself, and checked in with some of those mentors along the way, the decision became very clear and a lot easier to make. Never lose touch with people who truly know who you are and what your strengths are because they become invaluable resources even when you don't expect them to be.

What are a few things you wish you had learned in school about your career?

Well, there is a large part of me that wishes I went right into the nonprofit world out of college, but I tried law school, finance, and sales in between. I wish that someone would have told me that you don't have to have it figured out at 22 and also that it's okay to change your mind as many times as you need to until you're in the right job or on the right path. It's so common now for millennials to have several jobs over the course of a few years. It's not nearly as much of a negative as it used to be. But I will say, I would not be as good at my job now without the professional experience I got working in the private sector. There are huge benefits to trying a few things out to see what feels best before really settling in, and it's okay to do that!

What do you love about working in your industry?

I love that at the end of every day I can truly say to myself, I've made a difference today. It may not be a huge difference, and I also may be going to bed extremely tired and stressed out, but my organization has such a huge reach and I know the work we do is so important to so many millions of people that I can feel satisfied with that each and every day. That is honestly never something that I experienced working in the private sector. There is something so special about working for an organization that positively affects people every day; it really never gets old.

What do you think are emerging trends within your industry?

The nonprofit sector is finally coming on board with emerging trends in technology, and I've definitely seen improvements in the things that we can do out in the field, workflows, and analytics. Because technology trends tend to be costly as well, it takes a while for nonprofits to adopt them, but when they do, the organization really benefits.

What advice do you have for someone starting out in your industry?

I would say try it before you buy it, so to speak. A lot of larger nonprofits, mine included, offer wide-ranging internships for juniors and seniors in college. I think that is so important. With a lot of these jobs, you look at the description on paper and think, "Oh, I could do that, no problem!" But then when you get into it, you're in over your head or it's just the wrong fit. Interning with the organization and, even better, with a smaller department or job to what you think you want to do, allows you to really hone your skills and decide if it's right for you. I had an intern last year for 6 months, and she loved it so much and did really well and had a job working for me right when she graduated. She's all hired on, trained, and ready to start the fiscal year with us now. There's a huge sense of satisfaction for both of us, knowing that she's good at the job, she likes it, I've trained her, and she's not going to burn out.

What are the three most essential skills for success in your industry?

1. The absolute most important skill that I would not succeed without is organization. Since I work with so many schools and districts over two states, I have to constantly manage my calendar and my time. I have a paper calendar as well as my Outlook calendar (and obviously my phone), and I have a notebook for my to-dos and a separate one for notes. It's the only way I can stay on top of everything I have to do.
2. After that, it's the drive to be successful and the drive to impact as many lives as I can.
3. Then [it's] compassion. I meet people every single day that share the most unbelievable stories with us, and it's too important to meet them

(Continued)

(Continued)

where they are. I've had people tell me they didn't know salt was the same thing as sodium and that salt was heavily present in canned foods. You can never overestimate the knowledge people have, and you can never underestimate the power of what knowledge can do to their lives when you give it to them.

How has networking influenced your professional life?

Networking is very important for me, especially because of where I live; everyone knows everyone. School districts and officials are more connected than I would have ever imagined but not in the ways we see in the private sector. I don't find new people on LinkedIn; instead, it's by word-of-mouth references and personal introductions: old school but more personal.

How do you suggest someone stay up to date on your industry and remain competitive?

Believe it or not, Twitter has become a hotbed for nonprofits. It's an easy way to share successes and news as well as to connect with the community. I would also reach out to a nonprofit you're interested in and see if you can volunteer. We're ALWAYS in need of compassionate people that want to help.

INSIDER INSIGHT

LINDA J. SMITH, MARKETING DIRECTOR

What is your job description?

I am the marketing director for a large senior living community. We are a nonprofit organization (NPO) that has been in the community for 124 years. We specialize in senior living, nursing care, and short-term rehabilitation.

Describe a day in the life of your job.

No day is exactly as planned. As the marketing director, I am also responsible for admissions to the community. We run a large short-term rehabilitation program consisting of 130 rooms. This area of care is very transitional and needs daily monitoring. When census in rehab is low, marketing initiatives are directed toward hospitals and physicians. I also market heavily to the community for the rest of our continuum. I use print advertising weekly to keep our name at the forefront of the community. I also host weekly events on campus to get foot traffic in the door and make them aware of our services. I monitor a team of eight admissions counselors and also oversee the reception team as part of our customer service initiative.

What are the biggest misconceptions about your industry?

That as a senior living community, we simply wait for the people to come to us. The competition has gotten brutal in senior living. Many new organizations are popping up weekly. It is also imperative that running such a large rehabilitation business that we monitor our daily costs. In addition, we need to stay on the cutting edge of programming and health care initiatives within the marketplace as well as Medicare rules and regulations.

What is the best professional advice you have received?

Be nice to your staff. I try very hard to empower my staff to be the best they can be without micromanaging them. I also frequently buy lunch for them as a treat or do special things to make them feel appreciated. My staff can make me look good, and I want them to know that I appreciate all they do on my behalf.

How have mentors influenced your career?

I had one boss before I took the job who spent the time to educate me on the industry and teach me all she knew. I try to mirror that with all of my current staff. I have had other bosses that come at 9:00 and leave at 4:00, while I was continuing to work well past those hours. I think it is important that your staff know you are willing to work as hard and as long as they do, even as the boss.

What are a few things you wish you had learned in school about your career?

I do not have formal training in my field, so this is a difficult question to answer. That being said, it reflects the fact that on the job training is probably the best training you can receive.

What do you love about working in your industry?

I love that the health care industry is changing so quickly. There are always opportunities for new ideas and growth. Also, working in the senior industry I obviously love talking with the seniors and hearing their stories. Each one has something unique to tell, and you just have to take the time to listen.

(Continued)

(Continued)

What do you think are emerging trends within your industry?

As the baby boomers become seniors, their expectations are significantly different than has been seen in the past. They expect luxury and only the best for themselves and their parents. They are very driven to find the best level of care for the lowest cost. They also want to stay in their homes as long as possible and come to long-term nursing care only when they have no other choice. We have had to refocus some of our areas of care to accommodate their needs and eliminate some of our lower levels of care that were no longer necessary.

What advice do you have for someone starting out in your industry?

Immerse yourself in the industry. Get to know the trends and the competition in your area. Talk to as many people as you can, and network with your competition. Your community may not be the answer for everyone, but to be able to educate a consumer and refer them to the right place is a task that does not go unnoticed by the consumers. Become a resource for the community instead of just a service for them.

What are the three most essential skills for success in your industry?

1. The ability to change your agenda quickly
2. The time to put in the hours needed
3. The resources to stay on top of the ever-changing health care industry rules and regulations

How has networking influenced your professional life?

As a leader in our local community for 124 years, the expectation of my job is that we remain a mainstay in the community. We sponsor and host many community events just for goodwill purposes. Networking with the competition is also critical to my job so that I am aware of what they are doing and providing, which we may not be. Also, you can see what is working for the competition and where their census is to stay on top of the trends.

How do you suggest someone stay up to date on your industry and remain competitive?

Read the local paper daily! There is a ton of information in the local paper about different industries and the community, which helps you see where you can fit in. For my industry, it is to receive all of the Medicare updates by the government so we know about changes.

NONPROFIT JOBS: BY THE NUMBERS

$54,130 Annual median salary in 2016 for a fund-raiser

Annual median salary in 2016 for a marketing director **$127,560**

$105,000 Annual salary of training and development managers

A bachelor's degree is required.

Careers in nonprofit industries are expected to remain stable over the next decade, but the job outlook for fund-raisers and marketing managers is expected to increase by 9%.

Careers in nonprofits account for 11.4 million U.S. jobs, which is 10% of all private sector jobs.

Source: Adapted from the U.S. Department of Labor (2016).

SKILLS NEEDED FOR NONPROFITS

Each role in an NPO requires slightly different skills, especially depending on which area you decide to pursue. However, in what follows are some of the general skills one should have in addition to their specialized skills. This is not an exhaustive list. This list was composed using content from current job postings and the U.S. Bureau of Labor Statistics (U.S. Department of Labor, 2016).

Attention to detail

Basic computer skills (Microsoft Office Suite)

Commitment

Dedication

Organization

Passion for the cause

Strong written, verbal, and nonverbal communication

Teamwork

JOB SEARCH TERMS

The following is a preliminary list of job search terms that can be used to jump-start your own job search in nonprofits.

Community outreach

Development

Engagement

Fund-raising

Marketing

Nonprofit

Project coordinator

Retention/recruitment/membership

SKILLS

With each professional experience, you should gain new skills. You should also gain skills in your classroom coursework throughout college. For example, you know how you (or your classmates) complain about group projects? Those group projects help cultivate your "soft skills" that will inevitably influence the type of coworker you become. Or maybe you don't understand how your knowledge or expertise in an area can be fairly assessed through only a midterm and final exam? This type of teaching style focuses on "hard skills" that measure your knowledge base.

Skills coupled with your experience are the two factors that land you a job. There are many people and scholars who argue that your skills alone can predict your ultimate success. This chapter will discuss the different skills needed to help you start and build your career in a mass communication industry. Let's start by talking about hard and soft skills, since these two seem to get the most attention. So, what is the difference between hard and soft skills?

HARD SKILLS

Hard skills are specific, teachable abilities that can be measured. Typical hard skills include math, reading, foreign language, and computer skills to name a few. Hard skills are quantifiable—thus, the reason that degrees and certificates are valued and required for jobs. A degree serves as the measure indicating that a person has successfully developed their hard skills in a particular area. Hard skills are often listed within job postings and on résumés to indicate what is expected and whether or not an applicant is qualified.

Hard skills require the use of the left brain, or logic center, and are measured through IQ. Hard skills are typically learned in school and through mediums like books. One advantage to hard skills is that they often have a direct path to success, and it is clear when one is progressing. For example, once you master algebra, you move on to geometry, then precalculus, then calculus, and so on. It is similar for learning a skill like web design or hypertext markup language (HTML). Web design and HTML do not require situational knowledge: You either have the skills to do the job or you do not. The rules for hard skills remain the same no matter what. Another advantage of hard skills is that they can be learned through training, whereas soft skills are typically learned through trial and error. Hard skills are required for many careers in mass communication but are best accompanied by strong soft skills since most careers within mass communication are people-driven.

SOFT SKILLS

In contrast to hard skills, soft skills use the right brain, often referred to as the emotional center. They also cannot be measured, are not quantifiable, and operate with rules that change based on situations (Han, 2015). Soft skills can be cultivated within school but are mostly learned through experiences and trial and error—hence, the importance of participation in group projects, team involvement, extracurricular activities, and attendance at social events. Each one of these helps people learn, understand, and practice their soft skills. Often, soft skills are also listed on job applications along with hard skills but are harder for job candidates to demonstrate on paper. This is a main reason why interviews are such a vital part of getting a job. During an interview, your soft skills are being evaluated after determining that you have the relevant hard skills—at least as indicated on your résumé.

A major difference between hard and soft skills is that with soft skills, the rules are fluid. Think about how you behave when you're with your friends at a party, versus at work, versus at home with family. In each one of these situations, you demonstrate different aspects of communication. You may be more outgoing with your friends, more professional at work, and more emotional among family. You also likely dress differently and display different mannerisms in different situations as well. The way you adjust to your surroundings demonstrates the expertise of your soft skills. It is probable that you've met someone who does not seem to understand how to behave in certain situations, and this is likely because they have fewer soft skills than you. However, you might still be wondering what soft skills are. Here's a list for you (Han, 2013).

Self-Management Skills

These 10 skills address how you perceive yourself and others and how you manage your personal habits and emotions.

1. *Growth mind-set.* Be able to look at challenges as opportunities to grow and improve yourself.
2. *Self-awareness.* Understand what motivates, frustrates, angers, and inspires you to know how different situations affect your actions.

3. *Emotion regulation.* Be able to manage your emotions at work so that you can think clearly and objectively and act accordingly.
4. *Self-confidence.* Believe in yourself and your ability to accomplish things.
5. *Stress management.* Be able to stay healthy, calm, and balanced during challenging times. This includes knowing how to reduce your stress level to increase your productivity.
6. *Resilience.* Be able to bounce back from disappointments, setbacks, and failures and continue to move forward.
7. *Forgiveness.* Be able to forgive yourself and others so that you can move on and focus on your future goals.
8. *Persistence and perseverance.* Be able to remain dedicated despite challenges.
9. *Patience.* Be able to step back during a crisis to think clearly and take objective action.
10. *Perceptiveness.* Be able to pick up on unspoken cues and the emotional situations of others.

In addition to the 10 skills just discussed, people skills are essential. This is probably a term you've heard a lot of throughout your education. Statements like "it's not what you know, it's who you know" and other clichés about being good with people come to mind. But people skills are real, and they address how well you interact and work with other people. Generally, they are broken down into two types: (1) conventional and (2) tribal. Conventional skills are the skills you can find in most job descriptions and the skills you are typically assessed on during performance reviews. Tribal skills are the skills you won't find in job descriptions but are essential to your long-term career success. Here's a breakdown of the two types:

Conventional

1. *Communication skills.* Being able to actively listen and articulate your own ideas through written or spoken words
2. *Teamwork.* Being able to work effectively with people of different skills, backgrounds, personalities, and across industries
3. *Interpersonal relationships.* Being able to build trust, express empathy, and build relationships with people in your network
4. *Presentation skills.* Being able to effectively present your ideas and work to various audiences
5. *Meeting management.* Being able to lead effective, worthwhile meetings to reach productive results

6. *Facilitation.* Coordinating and soliciting opinions and feedback from various groups to find the best solution
7. *Sales.* Being able to get others to buy in to ideas, decisions, actions, or products
8. *Management.* Creating and motivating others of various skills and backgrounds
9. *Leadership.* Being able to define and communicate ideas that inspire others to follow through with dedication
10. *Mentoring or coaching.* Being able to provide constructive wisdom and guidance to help others further their careers

Tribal

1. *Managing upward.* Proactively managing your relationships with superiors to be positive and fruitful
2. *Self-promoting.* Subtly promoting your skills and work results to people of influence within your network
3. *Dealing with difficult personalities.* Being able to achieve results despite working with difficult people
4. *Handling difficult situations.* Being able to stay calm and objective despite challenges and unexpected events
5. *Navigating office politics.* Being able to understand and proactively and constructively deal with unspoken nuances in your workplace
6. *Influencing or persuading.* Being able to influence perspectives or decision-making while still allowing others to feel like they made up their own minds
7. *Negotiating.* Being able to understand the other side's motivations and leverage to reach a win-win result
8. *Networking.* Being able to be interested and engage in business conversations that motivate people to want to be in your network

The soft skills are what set people apart from others. You and another job candidate may be equal in terms of hard skills, but the reason one of you will get the job is most likely due to the development of your soft skills. While some people, especially those early in their careers, do not see the value in getting to know people, being nice, or socializing, those who embrace the development of soft skills see exponential improvement over time. When applying for jobs, the cover letter is your best opportunity to discuss your soft skills since typically these skills don't stand out on a traditional résumé.

Careers can be broken down into three main types: (1) careers that need mostly hard skills and few soft skills, (2) careers that need a roughly even mix of hard and soft skills, and (3) careers that need mostly soft skills. The careers that are primarily based on hard skills are technical careers, like a chemist. Careers that need a good mix of hard and soft skills are the more specialized careers within mass communication, like a web designer or producer. However, most careers in mass communication require mostly soft skills. Careers in mass communication are people-oriented. You have to understand people, read people, research people, and evaluate people for success in mass communication. Thus, having soft skills and some hard skills is vital for a career in mass communication. To evaluate whether or not soft skills are crucial to your career, answer these three questions (Han, 2015):

1. Are my abilities to work well and communicate with others essential to my performance review and promotion?
2. Are people in the same position as me well liked and promoted faster than me?
3. Does my ability to control my temperament at work affect my performance?

If all three of your answers are yes, then soft skills are very important to your career and you should spend time developing your soft skills.

INTERPERSONAL SKILLS

Interpersonal skills, a broad and deep soft skill, are also important to your career success. Interpersonal communication is the communication that occurs between interdependent parties, who have some knowledge of each other (Altman & Taylor, 1973). For example, interpersonal communication occurs between employers and employees, supervisors and subordinates, coworkers and clients. Interpersonal communication is a robust area of study because it occurs using a variety of channels and can help explain everyday phenomena including how romantic relationships begin and end, conflict, family relationships, and intergenerational communication. While entire books are devoted to interpersonal skills within the workplace, there are three main areas you should be aware of: (1) emotional intelligence, (2) self-disclosure, and (3) workplace relationships.

Emotional Intelligence

Emotional intelligence, particularly within the workplace, is a hot topic among employers and supervisors right now. Emotional intelligence, commonly referred to as EQ, argues that success is strongly influenced by personal qualities such as perseverance, self-control, and skill in getting along with others (Deleon, 2015). Employees with higher EQ are better able to work in teams, adapt to change, and remain flexible (Deleon, 2015). This is a primary reason why employers are putting so much emphasis on hiring employees with high EQ. The right hiring decisions can help preserve organizational culture and lead to more engaged and committed employees. Goleman (2005), who's written books about why EQ matters, presents five categories of emotional intelligence:

1. *Self-awareness*. A person who is self-aware understands their own strengths and weaknesses and how their actions affect others. People who are more self-aware are better able to handle and learn from constructive criticism.
2. *Self-regulation*. People high in self-regulation understand how to appropriately express and restrain their emotions, based on different situations.
3. *Motivation*. People with higher emotional intelligence tend to be more self-motivated. They are rarely motivated by material items and are very resilient and optimistic.
4. *Empathy*. Showing empathy and compassion helps people connect to each other on an emotional level. The ability to empathize helps people provide great service, so this is especially important in people-centric careers.
5. *People skills*. People who are emotionally intelligent can quickly build rapport with others and trust people who they work with since they enjoy and respect other people.

Self-Disclosure

In addition to emotional intelligence, people need to understand how much to share about themselves, to whom, and when. This is a concept referred to as self-disclosure. In the workplace, as opposed to within personal relationships, self-disclosures can be tricky because people want to maintain separation between their private and professional lives (Smith & Brunner, 2017). Self-disclosure refers to "interaction between at least two individuals where one intends to deliberately divulge something personal to another" (Greene, Derlega, & Mathews, 2006, p. 411), including revealing thoughts and feelings (Derlega, Metts, Petronio, & Margulis, 1993). Self-disclosure has multiple dimensions, including depth, which suggests self-disclosures range from trivial to intimate (Cozby, 1973). People often feel vulnerable revealing intimate disclosures (Altman & Taylor, 1973). Self-disclosing sensitive information at work may be particularly complex considering legal protections provided to the discloser (e.g., Health Insurance Portability and Accountability Act [HIPAA], Electronic Communications Privacy Act [ECPA]), which could influence how people manage their private workplace self-disclosures.

Research findings indicate that several factors influence why people disclose personal information in the workplace, including organizational culture (Smith & Brunner, 2017). Some organizations embrace a culture where coworkers feel like friends or even family, whereas other cultures try to prohibit sharing personal information with coworkers or supervisors. People also consider their relationships with coworkers and supervisors when deciding what or how much to disclose and also do a cost–benefit analysis of the potential risks and benefits about sharing personal information. In the workplace, when people feel their expectations for privacy have been violated, they are likely to take corrective actions including reporting the violation to human resources (HR) and confronting the violator, which can lead to other relational issues at work (Smith & Brunner, 2017). Thus, workplace relationships and an understanding of the pros and cons of workplace relationships are essential to manage your communication. As a word of caution, be careful what you share online, especially if your coworkers and supervisors follow you. Simply because you are not physically at work or sharing something during off-hours does not make it exempt from influencing your workplace relationships.

Workplace Relationships

Workplace friendships are part of personal career building and are important for organizations. Workplace relationships help people find out relevant organizational information, but they also increase creativity and make time spent at work more enjoyable (Rawlins, 1992). Peer relationships, or those between coworkers, are the most common type of workplace relationship. Peer relationships provide employees with emotional support and an alternative to traditional mentor–mentee relationships. Additionally, peer relationships provide intrinsic rewards for employees, buffer stress, and reduce job dissatisfaction and turnover (Kram & Isabella, 1985). However, workplace relationships can create stress for employees and create tension when not managed properly (Bridge & Baxter, 1992).

A main differentiating factor between workplace friendships from other types of relationships is voluntariness (Rawlins, 1992). Friendship, even in the workplace, cannot be forced upon people the way a relationship between a supervisor and subordinate can be. Friendships and romantic relationships at work develop by choice. Several other factors including proximity, shared tasks, supervisor behavior, personal life, and similarities influence the development of workplace relationships (Allen, 1977; Brehm, 1985; Eisenberg & Goodall, 1997; Fine, 1986; Odden & Sias, 1997). Sias and Cahill (1998) found that the development of workplace relationships, specifically friendships, experience three transitions: (1) from coworker or acquaintance to friend, (2) from friend to close friend, and (3) from close friend to almost best friend. These transitions were related to proximity, shared experiences, socializing, and the passage of time. Of particular relevance is the role that communication plays within workplace relationships since it is the workplace context that influences communication (Sias & Cahill,

1998). This information is relevant to you because if you are someone who needs friendship to feel comfortable and help you achieve success, you should pay close attention to the workplace culture when you are interviewing for a career in mass communication.

PERSONALITY

Another element that affects the success people can reach within their career is personality. Individual differences, including personality types, have been studied for decades and show that these individual differences do have significant impact on people's careers. As teleworking or working from home has become a requirement for many millennials and recent college graduates, scholars have started studying personality and teleworking to determine whether or not some personality types are better suited to remote working environments than others (see Smith, Patmos, & Pitts, 2015). So how is personality assessed, and what type of personality type are you?

The Big Five has had great success in explaining many aspects of life and career outcomes, such as subjective well-being, longevity, job performance, and leadership emergence and effectiveness (Judge, Ilies, Bono, & Gerhardt, 2002). The Big Five characteristics of personality encompass virtually all personality measures neatly into these factors: *openness, conscientiousness, extraversion, agreeableness,* and *neuroticism* (Goldberg, 1990). The Big Five have been found to generalize across almost all cultures and appear to remain relatively stable over time (Judge, Higgins, Thoresen, & Barrick, 1999). The Big Five, characterized next, are one of the most supported measures of personality. Understanding a person's personality can help determine the amount of success they will experience in certain jobs and is therefore why many employers make job candidates complete personality assessments prior to being hired. The Big Five is assessed using the NEO Five-Factor Inventory (NEO-FFI) scale, which can be found online.

Openness is characterized by divergent thinking and is strongly related to creativity (Judge et al., 2002). Furthermore, individuals who are high in openness are likely to have a rich and complex emotional life as well as be intellectually curious, behaviorally flexible, and nondogmatic in their attitudes (Costa & McCrae, 1992). Employees high in openness seek variety and tend to have more favorable attitudes toward learning, which may make them a satisfied teleworker (Clark, Karau, & Michalisin, 2012).

Conscientious people are associated with high levels of academic and vocational success due to their need for being well organized, scrupulous, and diligent (Costa & McCrae, 1992). Conscientiousness is also related to overall job performance; more conscientious employees tend to have better job performance evaluations than less conscientious employees (Barrick & Mount, 1991). Furthermore, conscientious people tend to be good leaders because of their tenacity and persistence (Goldberg, 1990).

Extraversion is a characteristic that is strongly related to social, energetic, and lively people (Judge et al., 2002). Extraverted people tend to prefer environments that are abundant with stimulation, social interactions, and activity (Clark et al., 2012).

Agreeable individuals are likely to be modest, cooperative, friendly, trustworthy, and helpful (Clark et al., 2012; Judge et al., 2002). Agreeableness is positively related to job performance, specifically in jobs that involve interpersonal interactions (Mount, Barrick, & Stewart, 1998). Furthermore, trust is an important component of teleworking success as well as cooperation: two traits that people high in agreeableness possess (Pratt, 1984).

The final component of the Big Five, neuroticism, is associated with a lack of emotional stability, insecurity, fear, and instability (Goldberg, 1990). People high in neuroticism are also described as anxious, depressed, or worried (Clark et al., 2012). Together, the Big Five can help both employers and employees alike find careers which emphasize their strengths and downplay their weaknesses based on the disposition of each person's personality.

CONCLUSION

In sum, skills are the true predictors of future career success, whether in mass communication or another industry. Learning what your skills are, how to improve weak skills, and match your skills to a career is essential to your personal success. Especially starting out in your career, taking time to inventory your skills can help set you apart from other job candidates and propel your career faster.

PREPARATION

You may already know exactly what type of job you plan to apply for, and you may still be deciding and keeping your options open. Or you may be earlier in your collegiate career and just beginning to think about your postgrad life. Either way, preparation is key for obtaining a job or internship. In today's society, people are accessible 24 hours a day, every day of the year. This is both a blessing and a curse. Want to know what it's like to work at a specific company? Websites like Glassdoor can tell you about salaries, company culture, and more. Curious how long the person interviewing you has worked at the company? LinkedIn can tell you that plus where they went to school and have previously worked. What this means for you is that you are also equally accessible. Thus, preparing yourself in addition to your credentials is crucial.

Understanding what personal branding is and how to build your brand is a great first step in your career because you lay out your own road map and help people understand who you are and what you're about. Then, your online presence should enhance and supplement your personal brand. Your portfolio is one way to demonstrate your brand's product. Finally, networking is how you continue to build, expand, and deepen your brand over time.

PERSONAL BRANDING

Believe it or not, you already have a personal brand. You may be thinking, "I haven't even thought of this before. How can I have a brand?" and you're only half right. Regardless of whether you have actively built your personal brand or not, it already exists in some form online. Before discussing personal branding, a quick understanding of the difference between image and reputation is needed, since the two concepts are frequently misunderstood but important to personal branding. Image is what you do to influence what others think about you. Reputation is the sum of what others say or think about you. The difference between the two may seem subtle, but reputation is cumulative, and that is a key differentiating factor (Wilcox, Cameron, Reber, & Shin, 2013). With regard to personal branding, you are building your image, which influences your reputation, or how others perceive you based on your branding.

Personal branding is the practice of people marketing themselves and their careers as brands. Think about when you go into a store to buy a specific product. You walk to the correct aisle and see multiple options available. How do you decide? Aside from the price, the packaging is what draws you in. You pick up one brand, read about it, and either decide or compare it against another until you select only one. As a recent college graduate on the job market, you are the item on the shelf waiting to be chosen. Personal branding is your packaging. Take a minute to think about some of your favorite brands. Why do you prefer a brand like Nike over Adidas? Or Chipotle over Qdoba? Wendy's versus McDonald's? Whatever your preference, there is a direct competitor out there, so how do you differentiate between the two? It might come down solely to the price, or maybe the quality, the source, production, or how one brand treats their employees compared to another. The point is you have learned this information about brands over time. Brands have communicated with you. Personal branding is your chance to communicate with others about yourself.

The first step to create your personal brand is to brainstorm. Who are you? What makes you unique? What are your career goals? How do you want to be known? Answering these questions will help you conceptualize your brand. Maybe you're an expert at something, or maybe your cultural background gives you unique insight into today's trends, or maybe you have more experience than other people your age. The brainstorm is not a time to judge you harshly or put yourself down. It is the time to really consider what makes you great. If you can't articulate why you're the best, then how can someone else know? The brainstorm will help you develop your brand. During the brainstorm phase, you should also set goals and create a personal vision and mission for your brand that describes what you do and whom you serve (Schwabel, 2009).

After you've brainstormed, conduct an online audit for yourself. Google your first and last name, and see what comes up. Then, try additional combinations like your name plus your hometown, high school, college, and groups you are affiliated with. Take inventory of everything that is accessible about you. Is your Facebook profile or Twitter one of the first things to come up? Write that down. Is your home address and phone number attainable? Be aware of this for privacy purposes. Were you mentioned in a local police blotter for something you did as a teenager? Make sure this doesn't come up, and if it is not avoidable, be ready to explain. Maybe you searched your name, and nothing about you specifically came up. I can relate. My name is Stephanie Smith, and if you type that into Google, you get approximately 100 million results. Knowing how easy or hard it is for people to find information about you is powerful and an opportunity waiting to be seized. You need to be able to conduct a successful online audit of yourself so that you can demonstrate your ability to do this for future clients.

The third step, after brainstorming and doing a personal online audit, is to start building your brand. One of the best ways to do this is through a personal website. Creating a personal website is one of the best ways to get noticed in online search results (Hyder, 2014). Here's the good news: You do not have to be a master web developer or coder to make a great personal website. WordPress, Weebly, and several others let you host your site for free and offer hundreds of design templates to choose from. Your website should be a reflection of yourself and your goals. If you're aiming for a creative career, build your website to highlight your designs, photos, or pieces of work. If you want to be a writer, use your website as your first impression. The most important thing about your website is that it's a central information station for people to learn more about you and your brand. Your website should at the very least include a home page, a page about yourself, and examples of your work. If you want to include additional information, like a blog perhaps, feel free, so long as it is in line with your brand.

The last major step is to maintain and expand your brand. You've spent a lot of time brainstorming and creating an image; now you need to use it. Your brand should carry through everything you do. Link your online profiles to your website, make a business or contact card with your site, and update your information regularly. Then, find ways to produce value, and be purposeful in what you share (Hyder, 2014). There is so much "noise" or irrelevant and mundane information online. You don't want to just be noise. Create or curate content that is in line with your brand. Every post, photo, and link you share contributes to your personal brand. This includes things that you retweet. In today's hostile online environment, you want to be very careful what you post and share online. Now that you understand what you want to be known for, you can be strategic with what you share online to enhance your personal brand.

One important disclaimer is this: This is not an activity about removing your personality from your online presence. Creating a personal brand is a way for you to integrate your personal and professional lives into one cohesive image. There is still an opportunity for you to share your social life without coming across like someone perpetually on spring break. Do not mistake a personal brand as something stuffy and contrite. The best personal brands are genuine and authentic representations of people.

ONLINE PRESENCE

Throughout your high school and college careers, you've likely been lectured a time or two about your online presence. Teachers and professors like to use scare tactics explaining that one inappropriate post could follow you around for the rest of your life and cost you a potential job. Unfortunately, many young adults hear information like this and then when they are starting to look for jobs and internships eliminate any trace of them online. This is a big mistake.

Your online presence should contribute to your personal brand, and during times when you're on the job market, you should increase your use of social media channels. However, appropriate use is the key. You should remove any and all inappropriate photos or posts immediately. Anything racist, sexist, overtly political, or controversial should be removed. Although I wished it went without saying, any photos that show nudity (even a skimpy swimsuit), illegal activities, guns, or excessive behavior (think stacks upon stacks of hundred dollar bills with revolvers on top) should also be removed. But pictures from vacations, study abroad, social events, family occasions, and your lifestyle overall can remain. These photos help illustrate who you are and what makes you a unique and interesting person. You can easily clean up or "professionalize" your social media channels without removing them entirely. Employers are looking for you online, and it's more suspicious to be completely unknown online than it is to be in a picture eating a turkey leg at a football game. So let's discuss some best practices for each online medium.

LinkedIn

If you're not already on LinkedIn, you should be. LinkedIn is a free online professional networking website, with over 400 million users (LinkedIn, 2016). It enables users to build their professional identities online and stay in touch with colleagues and classmates while also discovering professional opportunities (LinkedIn, 2016). On the site, you create a profile that should include a professional headshot; the contents of your résumé; and additional information such as courses you have taken, a summary about yourself, publications, honors, awards, skills, and organizations with which you affiliate. Then, you can connect with other people to build your professional network. When you get a new job or update your profile, your network will be notified and vice versa. A good LinkedIn profile can help ensure the good work you do is publicly recognized and that others know how to reach you with relevant opportunities.

It is estimated that LinkedIn usage is especially high among bachelor's degree holders and those with advanced degrees as well as with high earners or those making at least $75,000 per year (Shin, 2014). LinkedIn also tends to skew higher in average age of users, which means that people with more experience are using the site heavily. What this means for you is that the people in hiring positions are looking for you on LinkedIn. It is estimated that 98% of recruiters and 85% of hiring managers use LinkedIn to find and vet job candidates (Shin, 2014). Building and enhancing your LinkedIn profile is easy. Here are five steps to get you started (Shin, 2014):

1. *Make a findable and visually appealing profile.* Your name and picture are what people see online, so make it worthwhile. Use a professional headshot, and take advantage of the headline. Think of the headline as the search terms you want to be associated with.

2. *Use your profile to showcase everything that doesn't fit on your résumé.* Take advantage of what LinkedIn offers, and fill out everything. Go beyond just listing your job title and company; add a description. Upload links to your work, and state results where possible. Try and fill out every single relevant section.
3. *Strategically connect with others.* Use LinkedIn to connect with existing professional and personal contacts including friends, classmates, former coworkers and supervisors, and even your friend's parents. Professors are also great to connect with and solicit for a recommendation, since they can speak to your work ethic. Unless you can find value in connecting with someone you don't know, try to keep your connections to people you've met or done business with.
4. *Snoop through your network.* Once you have built your network, use it! Snooping will help you find contacts in specific industries and with specific organizations. It can help you get hired and help you make hiring decisions.
5. *Stay active on the site.* As with most things, LinkedIn is what you make of it. If you use it regularly, you will remain current and relevant on the site. Remind your network of what you're doing and that you're doing it well through posts and updates. Using LinkedIn will also help your network continue to grow over time.

Twitter

Right now, if you have a Twitter account, you're likely using it to post funny tweets and keep up with favorite friends, celebrities, and news outlets. However, when you begin to search for a job and transition to a full-time professional environment, Twitter can become a more powerful tool. If you do not already follow industry leaders and influencers, this is a perfect time to start, especially since 83% of the world's leaders are Twitter users (Smith, 2016). Follow leaders and then retweet what you find interesting or relevant from them. This will help your Twitter presence grow but also increase your opportunity to be noticed by influencers. Beyond networking potential, Twitter can also be used to find better content, help you get known within your field, and even help you get a job.

If you want to find better content on Twitter, look for lists, rather than following hashtags (Herman, n.d.). Lists allow you to group together people and have all of their tweets come in on one separate feed. This can help you sort information and find things more easily, similar to a Google alert but on Twitter. Don't be shy either. If there's an area of interest to you but no list, start your own. Starting your own list is one way to help become known in your field. Other ways to become more well-known and build your personal brand on Twitter include curating your own content. So rather than just reposting an article, explain why you find it interesting (Herman, n.d.). You can also initiate polls on Twitter to find out what other people think and make commentary based on those results. However, to get known, remember that it's not simply about the number of followers you have. You want people to see your name and instantly recall what you're all about, so consider quality over quantity in terms of followers (Herman, n.d.). Finally, Twitter really can help you get a job, as hard as that may be for some of you to believe. Twitter and lots of Twitter accounts operate like a job board. If you tried searching "marketing jobs," you would find different accounts with potential opportunities to follow. Since you can follow specific companies on Twitter, you can also learn about jobs that way. Many organizations post job opportunities exclusively to Twitter, so this can be a very fruitful option.

Facebook

Facebook is often considered the father or grandfather of social media. Today, high school and college students, parents, and even grandparents use the app daily. Companies, blogs, organizations, and private citizens all use it for promotional and personal reasons. Thus, the Facebook waters are murky. Is it a tool solely for keeping up with people's personal lives? Or is it a professional powerhouse? The answer is both, but for you, it depends. Like I explained earlier, if you are nowhere to be found on social media, it is suspicious to potential employers. So, with regard to Facebook, rather than delete your profile when you're job searching, you can take steps to clean it up. Your profile picture should be appropriate, which means no alcohol, tobacco, nudity, or offensive language or clothing. However, appropriate does not mean it cannot be fun and reflective of who you are. There is no reason to remove your personality, but you also should think about how easy it is to pass quick judgment and misinterpret information on Facebook. The same thing goes for status updates: past, present, and future. Although you may lock down your profile, that does not ensure that previous status updates of a questionable nature cannot still be found. You are best served to delete them rather than run the risk of losing an opportunity. If you want to, Facebook can be used for professional networking and job searching, similar to other social media sites. Some people choose to keep their Facebook usage and connections strictly personal, which is, of course, your choice, but if you want to use it for professional purposes as well, it is possible.

E-Mail

E-mail requires a brief discussion since it is one of the fastest and most commonly used tools to contact employers and for employers to contact you. First, make sure your e-mail is professional. I teach about 100 students per year, and at least 10% have inappropriate e-mail addresses such as "hotgirl123" or "modellover" and even "meathead456," and I'm not making these up. Your e-mail address should be professional and simple. It's best to use some iteration of your name or initials so that people can recall it and there is less margin for error.

Second, your university e-mail address may expire the day you graduate, or you may have to pay a fee to have it extended. If you're not aware of these rules, or haven't planned ahead, there's a chance you're sending out an e-mail address to employers you may not have access to by the time they contact you. A great solution is to create a Gmail account and forward your university e-mail there, so you're getting everything in one place. Then, there is no worry that things will not reach you. Finally, remember that e-mails, no matter when you sent them or what your e-mail address was at the time, live on forever. If you do not want something to be saved, then don't put it in writing. Always refrain from using offensive language and sending offensive content. Also, be aware of the personal information you share via e-mail. Your e-mail signature does not need to include your home address, for example. Instead, it should state your name, any affiliations you want to include, maybe a phone number, and your e-mail address. Here's what mine looks like for reference:

> Stephanie A. Smith, PhD
> Assistant Professor
> Department of Communication
> Virginia Tech
> stephasmith1@gmail.com

The biggest takeaway with e-mail is that people expect you to use it correctly. This includes responding to e-mails in a timely manner (within about 24 hours); being polite; and being professional, even when not discussing professional things. E-mail is not the correct medium to share information you would not feel comfortable sharing publicly.

PORTFOLIOS

A portfolio is a compilation of your work. It is used to demonstrate your skills to employers and clients since a résumé alone is rarely sufficient. In creative industries, such as advertising, web design, graphic design, and writing-based careers, a portfolio is vital. However, portfolios can and should be made for any industry. Portfolios can be made online, electronically in pdf format, and as a hard copy. Usually, a combination of both is best so that you can direct people to your online portfolio, but bring a hard copy with you on an interview or to a client meeting. Here is what to include in your portfolio:

- *Title or homepage.* Welcome people to your website or portfolio with something that is both representative of your work and visually appealing. This is their first impression, so you want to make it a good one.
- *About me section.* A traditional résumé and cover letter rarely allow you to tell your full story. Include a one-page section about yourself that

gives you the opportunity to explain your background and your work in greater detail. This is a perfect place to explain why you want to work within a specific industry, what motivates you, and your overall style. This should not be tailored to a specific job or organization. It should be general about you. Save the tailoring for your cover letter.

- *Résumé with contact information.* You should include a pdf full résumé in your portfolio. This résumé should be your general version and also not tailored to a specific organization or job. It should be all inclusive of your work and experience.
- *Projects and any relevant results or outcomes.* This is the meat of your portfolio and your chance to show off. Include anything you've done that you're proud of and a brief description of the objectives for the project and the outcomes. For example, in public relations (PR), gathering media attention is always a desired objective. If you wrote a press release for a client, include the release, and then include links to the various news outlets that picked it up. Be as specific as possible, and make this section very visually appealing.
    - *Important note:* If you did something on a team or for a group project, you can absolutely still include it. You'll want to describe the project and your contribution along with the final product.
- *A reference speaking to your work or testimonials from clients.* If you have a reference from a former boss, internship director, or professor, put it in your portfolio. If you've worked with clients or classmates who can speak to your skills and abilities, you can also include their thoughts as testimonials. This really helps tie everything in your portfolio together.

In sum, start putting together a portfolio. Include work you've done in your courses and from any internships or jobs. Have fun with building your portfolio, and use it as a humble brag about your work.

12

EXPERIENCE

One of the biggest complaints that first-time job seekers have is that they don't have enough experience. Most entry-level jobs require 1 to 3 years of experience. This can be frustrating to recent college graduates because it feels like you don't have enough experience and no one is willing to give it to you. However, you're not a hamster on an endless wheel. You likely already have some valuable experience, and if not, obtaining relevant experience is achievable. The trick is in how you package yourself, your skills, and your experiences in your job applications.

INTERNSHIPS

Internship experience is highly valued by employers. In fact, 81% of employers have found that new hires with relevant internship experience are better prepared than those without internships (Lebel, n.d.). However, students often perceive the role of an intern as a glorified personal assistant who exists solely to carry coffee and make copies. While this may be partially true, depending on where someone interns, internships are now a necessity to not only gain experience but to land a job after college.

So, what is an internship? An internship is a fixed term of temporary employment with an organization. Internships can last for 6 weeks, several months, or even 1 year. An internship must either be paid or count for course credit; otherwise, it is volunteer work. It is also illegal in many states for a position to be labeled as an internship if a person is not paid or does not receive college credit. Internships are not relegated to college students. Many organizations, including the National Basketball Association (NBA) and the National Hockey League (NHL), require interns to have college degrees already. This allows the interns to work full-time schedules and have the flexibility to work additional hours on game days. There are also many organizations that offer internships to high school students. Thus, getting an internship can often be as difficult and competitive as landing a full-time job. However, internships typically do not carry the same workload or time commitment that a full-time position requires. In fact, employers are urged to allow short shifts (about 4 hours) and flexible scheduling options to maximize the use of interns (Ricardo, 2015). Internships exist within virtually every industry and are extremely popular in mass communication fields; although some fields also offer apprenticeships. The biggest difference between an internship and an apprenticeship is that an apprenticeship trains someone to become a master within an industry, whereas an internship seeks to expose people to an industry-at-large. Regardless, both internships and apprenticeships exist to provide young adults with relevant career experience.

There are many reasons to obtain an internship. One reason might be that your school or major requires you to complete an internship before graduating. This is becoming the norm at many universities due to the value interning brings to students and employers. A bigger reason to get an internship is to gain experience. Experience is the number one reason students get internships. Additionally, internships provide exposure to industries, which can also be invaluable to college students preparing to graduate and enter the full-time workforce. Internships provide opportunities to experiment with careers that match your individual and academic interests (Loretto, 2016). Since many employers list previous internships as a requirement for their new hires, getting an internship is crucial to professional success postgraduation (Loretto, 2016). Thus, it is recommended that students get more than one internship throughout their collegiate career. Internships help you see what it is like to actually work within a specific field and evaluate the types of jobs that you are both qualified for and interested in performing on a daily, full-time basis.

Internships also help college students develop essential knowledge and skills, which increase their opportunities for getting hired (Loretto, 2016). Employers view internships as a way to train and assess the skills of interns, who often become employees. Therefore, it is critical that as an intern, you bring your best work and best professional attitude every single day (Loretto, 2016). Internships are when you will begin to understand workplace dynamics—something that cannot be taught in a classroom. It is also during an internship where you learn through observation by watching others and sitting in on meetings, partaking in client conversations, and assisting with projects. While internships are valuable to you, as an intern, they are equally as valuable to employers. Many employers report viewing interns as a pool of potential job candidates (Loretto, 2016). Bringing in previous interns as full-time employees helps make for a seamless transition and often leads to higher retention rates (Loretto, 2016).

Student interns can cultivate valuable and fruitful relationships while interning. Their internship supervisors can serve as a future reference and their fellow interns begin to build a professional network among like-minded people. It is during an internship when students begin to build their own network with people outside of their immediate proximity. Of additional importance is the bridge that an internship builds between the collegiate lifestyle and the full-time working world. During an internship, your social habits shift since your network is expanding. This helps you learn what your postcollege lifestyle will be like, which is important to your inevitable job search.

By now, if you didn't already know, you clearly understand the importance and value of an internship. But how do you get one? Well, it is a competitive market since almost every college student is also looking for an internship. But it is most certainly a possible task because interns provide such a great benefit to organizations. A first step should be the career services office at your institution. Many times local organizations solicit their internship opportunities exclusively with colleges and universities. This gives you a head start right off the bat. Your school's career services office can also provide you with guidance about your résumé and cover letter to help you find the best fit for an internship. Some departments will even conduct mock interviews with you so you should be taking advantage of this resource.

Another way to obtain an internship is to understand the selection process. With internships, there is not one sole criterion that lands you the opportunity (Coco, 2000). It is not based only on your grades, only on your major, or only on past experience. Instead, interns are usually selected based on the specific skills that can address an organization's need and leadership potential including consideration of extracurricular activities and attitude (Coco, 2000). However, it is not just the organization that makes the selection. You, as an intern, should pay close attention to where you apply and why. Not all internships are created equal, and some will be mostly administrative while others will be more creative and perhaps fulfilling. You should utilize the time during an interview wisely to gather information about your day-to-day responsibilities and expectations. Then, assess the information you have been given to determine whether or not this position is the best fit for you. While it is challenging and often difficult, you can and should politely decline any opportunity that is not best for you.

VOLUNTEER WORK

Internships are not the only way to gain valuable experience. If you are really in a pinch or want to positively influence your experience within a certain industry, consider volunteering. Volunteering is a donation of your time and skills to help a specific organization—usually a nonprofit organization (NPO) or community organization. Volunteers are always needed to help with administrative tasks, community outreach, fund-raising, event planning, and general publicity. Since NPOs and community organizations rely on volunteers, the opportunities for involvement are plentiful.

Volunteering is a great way to gain experience and build your network. Plus, you have the added benefit of helping an organization you are passionate about, which offers many intrinsic and psychological benefits. Volunteering also helps you get involved within your community. This is especially helpful when you are job searching because you can make valuable contacts with people in various industries and organizations. A great way to gain experience through volunteer work is to help with a special event or project. This is a good idea because it is a fixed period of time where your help is required. It does not indefinitely lock you in. Plus, you know that at the end of the project or event, you will have tangible results. Being able to tie your direct experience to measurable or visible results is a huge advantage when you're on the job market. For example, if you help plan an event, you can report the event attendance and money raised, perhaps, and compare it against the previous year to demonstrate the value of your work. Or, you may help design informational materials for a new campaign, in which case you can include these documents in your portfolio and showcase your work to potential employers. Lastly, volunteering can set you apart from other job applicants, especially on paper. Through volunteer experience, you can demonstrate that you can effectively manage, meet deadlines, engage with the community, and perform any other skills you acquired (Jones, 2012).

In addition to building experience, volunteering can also help account for "lost time" or gaps in employment history. This is very helpful for people who graduate college and don't have a job immediately because it keeps them engaged and busy as well as refining and perfecting their skills rather than seemingly living at home and off of their parent's income. Volunteering can also help you if and when you decide to apply to graduate programs (Jones, 2012). Another hidden benefit of some organizations is loan forgiveness. However, not all organizations offer this, so be sure to do adequate research if you're looking for this type of opportunity. Two large organizations that offer loan forgiveness are the Peace Corps and AmeriCorps if you meet a certain amount of contract hours and other qualifications (Jones, 2012).

COURSE PROJECTS

Although you may not have 3 years of full-time work experience when you graduate college, you do have at least 2 years of specialized coursework that you have completed. Typically, college majors require about 2 years of courses in addition to your general requirements. This is experience. If you don't already list relevant courses on your résumé, you should certainly add that information. If you don't have room, then talk about the relevant courses you have taken in your cover letter. Some examples might be courses like media writing, graphic design, editing, and strategic planning classes.

In each of these classes, you've likely had to produce something to demonstrate your mastery of the material. Course projects are great examples of experience for you to leverage. Often, students forget about course projects or do not consider them relevant experience since it was required. Well, many schools require an internship to graduate, so what is the difference? Why is an internship considered experience but a project you spent weeks working on is not? There should not be a difference. Even if you worked on a group project, this counts as experience—not to mention that more often than not, working on a group project is harder than completing something solo. You should include any relevant course projects in your portfolio and on your résumé where appropriate. When talking about your experience from classes, be sure to highlight the specific skills you learned such as teamwork, time management, project management, writing, design, editing, and evaluation, just to name a few. This will help bolster your experience and make a compelling case for why you have the necessary skills to be hired.

PART-TIME WORK

Employers today are not naive to the fact that college is expensive. Thus, they are understanding about recent college graduates' need to have part-time jobs while simultaneously completing their degrees. In fact, college graduates with work experience are more attractive than those without (Life, 2013). The obvious problem, however, is that typically these part-time jobs are seemingly irrelevant to a student's career aspirations. It is your job to explain and demonstrate to employers that your part-time work experience was not only necessary but also valuable to building the skills and experience they are looking for in new hires.

Part-time work experience has various values, including the financial value since you receive a steady paycheck. However, part-time work experience has the potential to exponentially build your network. For example, if you are a server at a bar or restaurant, you might have regular customers. If so, use that opportunity to explain you're preparing to graduate or get more experience in a specific field. For all you know, they might have a great contact for you. You are also building your network simply by working with other people including your supervisor and coworkers. Remember, there are about six degrees of separation between everyone, so your coworkers and supervisors could be closely connected to someone who can offer you a full-time job once you graduate.

For the purposes of discussing experience, I'm going to assume you're working or have worked in a part-time role that is not relevant to your future career goals. But what you may not realize is that in these part-time positions, you have cultivated important skills that will help you in whatever full-time position you acquire postgraduation. For example, you might regularly deal with customers, which would help you have the experience necessary to work in an account management role. Or you might frequently manage multiple projects and priorities, which would help you in a project management position. You may have also gained experience solving problems and thinking quickly under unique circumstances, which can be great experience for sales roles. If you package your skills from your part-time experience properly, it can translate into valuable experience (Kennedy, n.d.). Part-time work experience also demonstrates time management skills, dedication, and commitment. However, you should try your best to obtain a part-time job that relates to your future career goals.

CLOSING TIPS FOR EXPERIENCE

What is most important to remember is that a paycheck does not equal relevant experience. If you want to work in public relations (PR), being a lifeguard or a nanny for the past 4 summers is not going to help you even though you had to work for financial reasons. Instead, look for other opportunities to build up your experience through internships, volunteer positions, and course projects; leverage your part-time experience as well. What employers really want are college graduates with experience, not just a degree. Any way that you can relate your previous work experience to the position you're applying will help increase your chances of landing a great job in mass communication postgraduation. If you don't connect the dots, then no one else will. It is up to you to package yourself as an experienced job candidate, and sometimes that requires creativity and out-of-the-box thinking. When applying, try to mirror the language used in the job advertisement on your résumé and cover letter when you explain your experience. Also, use your cover letter as an opportunity to tell an employer more information about yourself above and beyond what is listed on your résumé. The cover letter is a great time to discuss the experience you have working with others and cultivating your soft skills.

13

SEARCHING AND APPLYING FOR JOBS

Currently, unemployment rates are starting to improve after being the highest since the Great Depression (International Monetary Fund and International Labor Organization, 2010). However, for entry-level employees, it is still very difficult to obtain postgraduate employment because the job searching landscape is highly competitive. This chapter is designed to overview what job searching is, strategies for job searching, and how to apply for jobs to stack the odds in your favor for landing a career in mass communication. Most important to realize, though, is that securing employment is directly related to both the job search behaviors that you perform and the amount of effort you exert during your job search (Blau, 1993). The right job will not fall into your lap when you're ready; you have to search.

JOB SEARCHING

Job searching is a difficult task that "requires the use of complex strategies, substantial self-control, and self-regulation skill" (Price & Vinokur, 1995, p. 192) and relies on a variety of communication skills and strategies. Similarly, job searching behavior refers to the specific activities that an individual engages in to acquire knowledge about employment opportunities (Bretz, Boudreau, & Judge, 1994). These behaviors include preparatory efforts such as gathering information and securing leads as well as active behaviors like applying to jobs and interviewing (Bretz et al., 1994). A job search is considered effective or successful based on the number of job offers received, as you might imagine (Saks & Ashforth, 1999). The process of job searching requires you to continuously manage your impressions through communication tactics such as cover letters and résumés, phone calls, events, and connections with professional contacts. Hence, it is important to build your skills, brand yourself, and enhance your experience prior to starting your job search, as has been discussed in previous chapters. The job search is your opportunity to bring all of that information and practice together.

You can job search using a number of communication channels such as websites (e.g., LinkedIn, CareerBuilder, Monster, Craigslist), recruiters, a personal network, advertisements, and word of mouth. There are three basic techniques people use to search for jobs: (1) formal means, (2) personal contacts, and (3) direct application (Granovetter, 1995). Formal means include communications such as advertisements and employment agencies. The defining characteristic of job searching through formal means is that you use the services of an impartial intermediary to find prospective employers. In contrast, job searching through personal contacts relies on the help of an individual who is personally known by you in a context unrelated to job searching, such as a friend or family member. Through a reliance on an interpersonal network, you are better able to connect and communicate with potential employers and have the opportunity to speak directly with decision makers (Mau & Kopischke, 2001). Finally, direct application techniques describe how you may contact a potential employer directly (online, via phone, or in person), do not rely on an intermediary of any sort (personal or impartial), and have not learned of the opportunity through an interpersonal contact.

The primary search strategy for recent college graduates is direct application through sending out résumés and applying to jobs through advertisements (Mau & Kopischke, 2001). Among all job seekers, it is reported that at least 60% of jobs are found through networking, or personal contacts (Doyle, 2014). Moreover, approximately 46% of job seekers made a direct application to the employer before getting hired, consistent with how recent college graduates search for jobs (Gordon, 2010). However, it is worth noting that new college graduates use more than one method to job search. Although sending out résumés is the primary search strategy, networking and recruiting agencies have been identified as secondary job searching strategies for college graduates (Holzer, 1987; Jensen & Westergard-Nielsen, 1987; Mau & Kopischke, 2001).

So why are so many people stressed about job searching? The process of job searching is riddled with discouragement, rejections, and setbacks, which presents challenges for job seekers (Price & Vinokur, 1995). For example, only 18% of Fortune 500 companies send e-mails when a position has been filled (Gordon, 2010). An additional challenge is the amount of time it takes to job search, often with little to no feedback throughout the process, increasing the uncertainty of job seekers. Between 1994 and 2008 the average job search took 5 weeks to complete (U.S. Bureau of Labor Statistics, 2014). By 2011, the average job search took 6 months; a quarter of job seekers spent up to 1 year job searching (U.S. Bureau of Labor Statistics, 2014). Currently, there are approximately 3.7 million people categorized as "long-term unemployed," which means they have been job searching for more than 27 weeks (U.S. Bureau of Labor Statistics, 2014). Together, the rejection or lack of feedback coupled with the time-consuming process of job searching creates challenges such as stress and increased uncertainty among job seekers that communication alone cannot overcome. You should be prepared for uncertainty and rejection as well as the time commitment it takes to find and secure postgraduate employment. Understanding the potential for disappointment can help you overcome rejection faster and maintain an optimistic outlook throughout your job search.

People who spend more time and effort on job searching find jobs faster (Wanberg, Hough, & Song, 2002; Wanberg, Kanfer, & Banas, 2000). Research on job searching and intensity has demonstrated that informal search methods, like networking, result in faster employment than formal methods of job searching (Granovetter, 1995). Individual differences may help you understand the different communication strategies used to job search. For example, a personality and job searching meta-analysis demonstrated that extraversion and conscientiousness were positively and significantly related to job searching, such that people higher in those two personality characteristics had better job search outcomes (Kanfer, Wanberg, & Kantrowitz, 2001).

In a field study specific to recent college graduates conducted over a 4-month time period, proactive personality was demonstrated to be an antecedent to successful job searching indicating that recent college graduates who have more proactive personalities have a shorter and more successful job search (Brown, Cober, Kane, Levy, & Shalhoop, 2006).

Finally, it has been reported that when job seekers receive helpful and supportive messages from others relating to their job search, their intensity of job searching increases (Holmstrom, Russell, & Clare, 2013), which may also help establish and manage expectations throughout the job search. Thus, for your job search, you should keep in mind that the more time you spend job searching could lead to faster results. Also, try to surround yourself with supportive people rather than friends who you may be competing with or people with negative attitudes.

JOB APPLICATIONS

Once you've found several jobs you want to apply for, you have to actually apply. Typically, even if you found a job through networking or an indirect method, it will still require an application. The good news is that this can be easier and less stressful than job searching. You may think that each application is the same and it should be a quick and easy task. However, the applications are vital and should be prepared and submitted with great care and attention to detail. One of the biggest misconceptions about job applications is that you can submit the same cover letter and résumé to every job. Do not do this. You want to tailor your résumé and your cover letter specifically to each individual position. As mentioned at the end of Chapter 12, you want to try and mirror the language in the job advertisement in your application materials. If an advertisement says that they want someone with Adobe Photoshop experience, you'd better have Adobe Photoshop on your résumé, assuming you have experience using the Adobe Creative Cloud. Oftentimes, employers use computer screening programs to sift through résumés, and these programs look for keywords that align with the job advertisement. If you had photo editing on your résumé instead of Adobe Photoshop, you might get sorted out. This is a simple trick that can have major payoffs.

A second thing to remember is that your cover letter should not be a duplicate résumé. You should not repeat any information in your cover letter that is already on your résumé. The two are meant to complement each other. Therefore, your cover letter is an opportunity for you to expand upon your résumé and tell the employer additional information about yourself. Some things to talk about in a cover letter include why you want to work for the company, your career aspirations, and your soft skills. If you know someone at the organization and were made aware of the job or encouraged to apply because of your contact, that information can also be included in your cover letter.

Third, be absolutely sure to follow all of the application directions. Incomplete applications or incorrect applications typically get thrown out without ever being reviewed. It is an easy way to weed out the pool of candidates. You do not want to be seen as someone who cannot follow directions, especially not for an entry-level position. In some way, your application submission is similar to a quiz to see how well you can respond and follow directions. This is the equivalent of free money. There is no reason that you cannot follow the application directions. For example, if the job advertisement asks for writing samples, be sure to include them. This is not optional. You should avoid the urge to include information that is not requested. Finally, many job advertisements include strict instructions *not* to contact the employer. This means that you should not e-mail the employer to inquire about the status of your application. You should not call the employer. You should not mail a hard copy of your application unless requested. You should not drop by the office to meet people and let them know you applied. Your parents or elders may encourage many of the things you should not do, but your safest bet is to strictly follow the directions of the job posting.

The final recommendation is to keep applying. Remember that you will have greater success in your job search if you use multiple methods to search for jobs and that your persistence with applications correlate to your interviews and job offers. Although you may find a position you feel is a perfect fit, do not stop searching and applying. Some employers are very slow with reviewing applications. It can take anywhere from a few weeks to a few months to be invited for an interview. On the flip side, you may apply and never get a confirmation e-mail or a formal rejection. There are millions of job applications living in a big cyber black hole somewhere, filled with people who were never notified they were not invited to an interview. This is exactly why you should keep applying and not give up until you have secured a job. While many people argue that job searching and applying is a full-time job, this is false. Job seekers who spend quality time job searching and applying have greater luck than those who apply for every job they can find. You really want to be thoughtful in your job search and in your applications to maximize your opportunities.

CONCLUSION

In sum, college graduates who use multiple communication methods to search for jobs have greater success in their job search and receive more interviews than new college graduates who rely on only one method of job searching (Mau & Kopischke, 2001). Additionally, although recent college graduates search for jobs using primarily formal means (Mau & Kopischke, 2001), you should consider networking and using third parties, like a recruiter or your school's career services department for help. Remember that job searching can be a difficult, unpredictable, and disappointing experience. Do not let this discourage you. Surround yourself with supportive people, and keep making industry contacts, building your experience, and applying. You will find a job.

INTERVIEWING

At this point, you've successfully branded yourself, searched for jobs, and have been offered an interview. Interviews are tricky because they are traditional yet also vary tremendously. Thus, while some people think the interview is a gateway to a job offer, a given, nailing an interview takes special preparation and practice. Interviewing can be broken down into three phases: (1) preparation, (2) execution, and (3) follow-up.

PREPARATION

Let's start with preparing for an interview. By the time you have been invited for an interview, an organization has already determined that, on paper, you have the required skills for the job. The interview is used to determine more information about your skills but also to learn more about you as a person. Interviews help assess whether you will fit into the company's culture, be a good coworker, interface well with clients, and the extent to which you can actively listen and articulate your thoughts. Also, remember that you are interviewing the organization as much as they are interviewing you. This is helpful when preparing for an interview since it can determine what type of questions you want to ask and what you want to take note of when you visit.

One of the first steps in preparing for an interview is to research the organization. You likely did this when you applied (at least you should have), but now you need to revisit that information and dig deeper. You should have a firm understanding of the organization's background, including why and when it was founded; the mission statement; and the products, services, and clients served where applicable. Another good idea is to read recent press releases and feature stories for insight on current happenings. Reviewing trade publications will also help you get an understanding of the organization's projected growth and stability. One of the biggest complaints of hiring managers is that many job candidates know very little about the company they are interviewing for (Smith, 2013). This is an easy challenge to overcome, and doing your homework on an organization can help set you apart from other candidates.

After you've done your homework on the organization, compare your skills and qualifications to the job requirements. Analyze the job description so that you clearly understand the knowledge, skills, and abilities required. Examine the hierarchy of the organization and the department in which you would be working. It is important to know how this position fits within the larger organization. Then, identify what the organization wants and needs, and figure out how you fit. While your first postgraduate job is extremely important to you, it's also extremely important to the organization. You need to remember this point; it's not all about you. It is your responsibility to focus on the hiring manager's needs to demonstrate how you can help them (Smith, 2013).

Now that you have studied the organization and the position, you can begin to craft your interview responses. This will be discussed in greater detail during the execution phase of the interview but needs to be addressed during the preparation phase, too. You can start to prepare responses by interviewing yourself. Ask yourself, "Why am I a good fit for this job?" Answer this question out loud. Practice how it physically feels to explain your qualifications. Practice the flow of your responses. Take stock of how you're saying things to polish your speech by removing "likes" and "ums" for a more prepared response. As a college student or recent college graduate, you have the advantage of a career services office that wants to help you ace your interviews. You should try to take advantage of mock interview opportunities to become more comfortable with your responses. It is important, however, not to memorize your response. Practice speaking about yourself and your skills naturally using a conversational tone.

Next, plan what you're going to wear, bring, and how you're going to get there. Personally, I tend to sweat a lot regardless of how nervous I am. During an interview, I sweat even more. Thus, I need to wear a dark colored shirt or jacket to minimize the appearance of sweating through my clothes. When I first graduated from college and was searching for a job, I was living in Chicago. Therefore, I had to always budget extra time into my commute for unforeseen traffic issues. You should carefully pick out your outfit at least a few days in advance to make sure you have enough time to clean and press your outfit. The best thing to wear is something neutral. A suit for both men and women is always a safe bet. Even if you know the organization you are interviewing with has a casual dress code, you should still err on the formal side unless you are strictly instructed otherwise by the organization. Do not wear any heavy scents such as perfume or aftershave, as some people are very sensitive to this. Also, make sure your shoes are polished and in professional condition because people take notice of small details like this. Both men and women should keep jewelry to a minimum. Men should also ensure that their facial hair appears well kept and trimmed. Women should keep their makeup as well as their nail polish conservative and natural in appearance. You want to dress to impress and as though you already have the job. Your overall appearance should be neat and clean.

When you are putting together your outfit, you should also put together the things you want to bring. A copy of your cover letter and résumé, as well as a pen and notepad, are must-have items. In fact, you may want to bring two copies of your résumé and cover letter just in case the interviewer doesn't have a copy nearby for reference. You should consider writing down your questions in advance to ensure you don't forget to ask something important in the heat of the moment. You might also want to print a copy of your directions just in case your phone dies en route or something else unexpected occurs. If you have a hard copy of your portfolio, you should also bring that with you and leave it with the interviewer.

The last important piece of interview preparation is knowing what type of interview you are having. These are some of the most common (Undercover Recruiter, n.d.):

Phone and/or Skype Interview

Phone and/or Skype interviews are often used as a preliminary interview before an invitation for an in-person interview. These can be conducted by someone in human resources (HR) to verify information or may be conducted by a hiring manager. Most of the time, these interviews are scheduled, but if you are called unexpectedly for a phone interview, it is acceptable to ask to schedule a time. During a phone or web interview, be sure that you are talking in a quiet room and not eating or drinking during the call. If you are being interviewed via Skype or some other web application, you'll also want to be dressed appropriately and have a neutral background like a white wall behind you. Be sure to turn your lights on too, and if you live with roommates or loud pets, consider going somewhere else for a web interview so that the potential for all distractions and interruptions is minimized.

Traditional One-on-One Interview

This is the most common type of job interview where a representative of the company interviews the interviewee. Typically, the interviewer is the person you would be reporting to if you got the job. The purpose of this interview is to get to know you and see how well your skills align with the job requirements. One-on-one interviews can be conducted in-person or via web applications.

Panel Interview

Panel interviews can be conducted either before or after a one-on-one interview. During a panel interview, several representatives of the organization, including HR, management, and other employees, simultaneously interview you. Panel interviews save time but also help get a collective opinion about the candidate. Each person on the panel typically asks the interviewee a question or two. Panel interviews are every bit as formal and important as one-on-one interviews and should be prepared for with the same attention.

Group interviews are typically used to prescreen potential job candidates. Unlike a panel interview, there is only one or two interviewers and several candidates. Group interviews can provide insight into how job candidates relate to one another. In other words, during a group interview you are under intense observation. Group interviews help candidates learn more about the company.

Lunch Interview

Lunch interviews are typically conducted as second interviews. During a lunch interview, you will dine with one or more representatives from the organization. This is helpful for both parties to get to know each other and gather additional information. This is an ideal time for you to ask questions, so you should prepare some in advance. However, you must be mindful of your manners. Avoid ordering anything too expensive, don't take leftovers home, and do not talk with your mouth full. Also, do not order alcohol even if the interviewer encourages it; that might be a test, so stick to water or a soft drink. It is understood that the organization is paying for the lunch.

EXECUTION

Now that you've been invited for an interview and understand which type of interview you're participating in, you can focus on your actual execution of the interview. There is a lot of advice about how to give a good impression during an interview, and most of that comes from being well prepared. During the interview, you have a responsibility to articulate your ability to not only perform the job, but also outperform any other job candidates. However, interviews also provide the opportunity to talk about things beyond the basic requirements of the position. Your interpersonal skills will make or break your interviewing abilities. You should remember that interviewers are not trying to trick or stump you. They are asking questions to get answers; that is their only motivation. So it is your responsibility to be an active listener and answer only what you are asked. There is no need to analyze their questions or overthink their motives, the way you might in a romantic or personal relationship.

Aside from further assessing whether or not you have the skills to do the job, during an interview you are being judged on how well you fit into an organization. The interviewer is trying to pinpoint not only whether you match up well with both the company and department's activities but also whether you'll complement the talents of your potential coworkers (Vogt, n.d.). You are also being evaluated on how well you understand the company and its purpose—hence, the importance of doing your homework before an interview. Similarly, you're being evaluated on whether or not you have the right mind-set to join the company. Employers look for knowledge of the company and the right attitude in job candidates, because when the organization fits with the candidate's career goals and when they have a matching attitude, retention and job satisfaction rates are higher (Vogt, n.d.).

There are two additional things employers look for during an interview, and they are how well you stack up against the competition and whether or not you portray that you want the job. Essentially, an interview is an exam that is graded on a curve. You will constantly be compared against the other job candidates. Therefore, if you really want the job, you should say it. But more than just talk the talk, walk the walk. Explain why you want it, how you fit, what you bring to the table, and how you can help the business grow over time.

Now let's talk about how to answer the intimidating interview questions. This seems to be the area that gives people the most anxiety due to the uncertainty surrounding what they will be asked. However, if you are prepared and qualified, you should feel significantly less anxiety. Nonetheless, you can still improve your answers using a few key strategies. First, be concise. This requires active listening during the interview. Answer only what you're being asked. This is hard for people who are not prepared enough or overprepared and reciting memorized, premeditated answers. Your answer should not be more than a few sentences. If the interviewer wants you to elaborate, he or she will ask for additional information. Second, provide examples as often as possible. Remember, the interview is not the time to recite your résumé. Instead, build upon the information in your résumé by giving examples based on your previous experience. This is a particularly good way to explain the results your work had. For example, you might want to explain that your social media campaign tripled the amount of Facebook followers for the company. Third, always be honest. Do not exaggerate. You were asked to interview because you have the desired skills and qualifications to work at the organization. You are an expert on yourself and your experience. Leverage both of these facts to give yourself confidence to help avoid the temptation of exaggerating or lying. Lastly, you want to ask great questions. The questions you ask indicate your interest in the job (Peterson, n.d.).

In addition to what you say, you are also communicating nonverbally during an interview. This is precisely why your appearance matters so much during an interview. Before you even begin to talk, you're already communicating. To stack the odds of nonverbal communication in your favor, you can focus on a few areas during an interview. The handshake says a lot about you, and it is your first impression with the interviewer. Your handshake should be firm, dry, and warm. It sounds funny, but trust me, your hands will be sweating. Keeping your hand in your pocket right before shaking can give you an inconspicuous chance to dry it off. Your posture similarly says a lot about you. During an interview, you should sit up straight and not hunch or slouch. This can also help keep you energized throughout your interview. While you're sitting up straight, you may be tempted to put your elbows on the table, but you want to avoid this. Try to minimize gesturing with your hands and touching your face during the interview. Ideally, you should keep your hands folded in your lap. Another trick is to mirror the body language of the interviewer. If they are sitting with their hands folded on the table, you can do the same. This helps ensure you're not communicating in a distracting way to the interviewer. Lastly, be conscious of your eye contact. Look the interviewer(s) in the eye, but don't stare. Avoid looking around when you're speaking, and keep your interviewer engaged in you through your eye contact. A great way to practice and polish your interview body language is to record a mock interview and watch it back (this is an option at many career centers), or practice speaking in front of a mirror (Martin, n.d.).

Here is a list of the top 50 most common interview questions (Smith, 2013). Thinking through your answers to these questions, as well as practicing them ahead of time, will help you feel more comfortable during an interview. Your comfort level directly influences your confidence, so there really is no harm in running through a few of these questions prior to an interview. Regardless, you should expect some of these questions to be asked during an interview.

1. What are your strengths?
2. What are your weaknesses?
3. Why are you interested in working here?
4. Where do you see yourself in 5 years? 10 years?
5. Why do you want to leave your current company (where relevant)?
6. Why was there a gap in your employment history?
7. What can you offer us that someone else cannot?
8. What are three things your former manager would like you to improve upon?
9. Are you willing to relocate?
10. Are you willing to travel?
11. Tell me about an accomplishment you are most proud of.
12. Tell me about a time you made a mistake.
13. What is your dream job?
14. How did you hear about this position?
15. What would you look to accomplish in the first 30, 60, and 90 days of this job?
16. Discuss your résumé.
17. Discuss your educational background.
18. Describe yourself.

19. Tell me how you handled a difficult situation.
20. Why should we hire you?
21. Why are you looking for a job?
22. Would you work holidays and/or weekends?
23. How would you deal with an angry or irate customer?
24. What are your salary requirements?
25. Give a time when you went above and beyond the requirements for a project.
26. Who are our competitors?
27. What was your biggest failure?
28. What motivates you?
29. What's your availability?
30. Who's your mentor?
31. Tell me about a time when you disagreed with your boss.
32. How do you handle pressure?
33. What is the name of our CEO?
34. What are your career goals?
35. What gets you up in the morning?
36. What would your direct reports say about you?
37. What were your boss's strengths and weaknesses?
38. If I called your boss right now and asked him or her about an area you could improve upon, what would they say?
39. Are you a leader or a follower?
40. What was the last book you read for fun?
41. What are your coworker pet peeves?
42. What are your hobbies?
43. What is your favorite website?
44. What makes you uncomfortable?
45. What are some of your leadership experiences?
46. How would you fire someone?

47. Describe your work ethic in three words.
48. What help do you need from the organization to be successful in this role?
49. How do you handle multiple projects or tasks simultaneously?
50. What questions do you have about the position or organization?

FOLLOW-UP

After an interview, it is customary to follow up with the interviewer to thank them for their time. Most likely at the end of the interview, they will discuss their time frame for hiring and their next steps. If they do not mention this, it is acceptable to ask. This will also help you determine the best way to follow up, especially if time is of the essence. A thank-you note following an interview is expected; however, the debate about a post-interview thank-you note is whether it should be handwritten or sent via e-mail. If you know they are looking to make a quick decision, there's nothing stopping you from getting into your car after the interview and writing the note and dropping it in their mailbox. Otherwise, try to write it the same day and get it in the mail ASAP. If you have poor handwriting, or really feel that an e-mail is appropriate, then send a thank-you e-mail. For example, if all of your correspondence has occurred via e-mail, then an e-mail thank-you would be acceptable. Here's a template for writing a post-interview thank-you note:

Dear [INSERT NAME],

Thank you so much for your time during our interview. I really enjoyed speaking with you and learning more about the [INSERT POSITION NAME] position. I am very interested in joining your team. Please let me know if you have any additional questions or would like more information. I look forward to hearing from you.

Thanks again,
[SIGN YOUR NAME]

Unfortunately, sometimes an interviewer will tell you a time frame and then not stick to it. So when is it okay to follow up? And how should you do it? First, be sure to ask the time frame, and understand it before you leave the interview. This will give you the answer to when it is appropriate to follow up. If they say they plan to make a hiring decision within 1 week and it's now been 2 weeks, you should follow up. When an organization gives you a time frame and then does not stick to it, give a few days or a week as a grace period, and then follow up.

Sometimes people get sick, have emergencies, or simply overestimate how quickly they will decide. It is not uncommon for hiring decisions to take longer than expected. Following up in this type of situation can help you relax and reduce your uncertainty. Plus, following up can provide an opportunity for you to remind the hiring manager why you're the right fit for the job. It is appropriate to follow up via e-mail, and it is the easiest way to do so. Sending a short but professional e-mail checking in on the opportunity is best. Here's a template:

Dear [HIRING MANAGER'S NAME],

I hope you're doing well. I wanted to check in on the [INSERT NAME OF POSITION] position that I interviewed for on [INSERT DATE]. I am still very interested in the position and think I would be a great fit for your team. I would greatly appreciate any update on the status of this search. Please let me know.

Thanks,
[INSERT NAME]

In sum, interviewing can be a very enjoyable, positive experience when you prepare properly. There is no reason that you should enter an interview feeling overly anxious or insecure. Utilize your resources, and remember that you are also interviewing the organization. Practice your responses, follow up, and remain vigilant in your job search. Even if you get invited for an interview with a job you are no longer interested in accepting, you should consider taking the interview anyway for practice. Like all things, without experience, you never improve. Talk to friends and family about their advice, go on lots of interviews, attend career fairs and engage in more informal interviews, and remember to have fun during this process. The interviewing stage is the final stage before accepting a job, so if you hate the organization during the interview, you probably won't like working there either.

15

CAREER SUCCESS STRATEGIES

Receiving a job offer is fantastic, especially as a recent college graduate. You should take a moment to soak in the achievement of obtaining a job and revel in your hard work for successfully completing a job search. But you're now entering another uphill climb to find success in your new position and with your new organization. You should begin to shift your thinking from obtaining a job to retaining your job, even before your first day of work. The transition from college to the full-time workforce is challenging, but with some preparation, it can be easier and lead to a faster adjustment period. Once you've adjusted to your job, paying special attention to your attitude and opportunities for continued learning experiences will help you find greater levels of job satisfaction. Finally, finding a mentor, as well as being a mentor, will provide exponential benefits for your career.

ADJUSTMENT AND ASSIMILATION

Anticipatory socialization is the process of forming expectations about a job and an organization prior to your first day in an effort to seamlessly transition into your new role (Dubinsky, Howell, Ingram, & Bellenger, 1986). You may have noticed during your interview process how people dress and bought new clothes accordingly. You may know that the organization you're joining uses Apple products, so you read up on that. You may have also noted other things like how employees communicate, interact nonverbally, and define their workspaces. Each of these things helps you determine how to behave when you arrive. This is anticipatory socialization. Through your observations and social interactions, you are taking mental notes and adjusting yourself so that when you begin working, you are accepted faster and seen as an insider, rather than an outsider or "new person."

Do not underestimate the power of learning through observation during your first few weeks and months in your new role. Starting a new job is overwhelming for anyone. You are faced with a steep learning curve, thrown into a new environment, and forced to adjust quickly if you want to be successful. Learning by watching others will help you adapt faster. Through observation, you can begin to understand the norms of an organization. For example, is taking a coffee break each morning considered acceptable, or is it frowned upon? Do people typically go out to lunch together, or do they eat quietly at their desks? Making these observations can help you integrate yourself into the various social situations of your job. Learning through observation can also help you understand proper meeting etiquette, how to communicate with supervisors and clients, and how to hold yourself and others accountable for their work.

Anticipatory socialization and learning through observation can also help you understand and assimilate to the workplace culture. Organizational culture is the values and behaviors that contribute to the unique social and psychological environment of an organization (Needle, 2004). Organizational culture represents the values, beliefs, and principles of an organization and emerges through an organization's history, market, employees, and leadership (Needle, 2004). This helps to explain why your experience at each job is unique and varied, even if you perform similar tasks. When interviewing, the employer is assessing your "fit" with the organization, which includes how well they think you will assimilate to the organizational culture. You are similarly assessing this. For example, anecdotal evidence suggests that millennials want to work for organizational cultures that do not have strict dress codes, allow working from home, and have open concept and collaborative workspaces. These variables are characteristics of the organizational culture.

CONTINUED LEARNING

Almost every single industry insider interviewed for this book discussed the importance of continued learning for success. As an emerging professional, you are already faced with a learning curve as well as being at the forefront of information having just graduated college. However, as you begin working full-time, your constant state of learning about the industry dissipates. Instead, you spend more time learning the ins and outs of your organization and the functions of your job. However, this is not considered continued learning. Continued learning refers to taking an interest in learning about your industry. A professional in advertising should be well versed in industry trends, regardless of whether or not they use these trends in their daily job responsibilities. Having a firm understanding of markets, trends, competition, and psychographics will enhance your overall knowledge that can positively influence your performance.

There are several ways to stay involved and continue learning once you enter the full-time workforce. Joining a professional association is one of the easiest and fastest ways to get involved. There are associations for communicators, marketing professionals, public relations (PR) practitioners, graphic designers, and broadcasters, just to name a few. The benefits of joining a professional association include a network of other professionals with varied experience levels at your fingertips; invitations to events; opportunities for awards and recognitions; and continued learning opportunities such as luncheons, lectures, and workshops. Joining a professional association can also provide you with an opportunity to be of service to your industry through an administrative role or by assisting with a special project. Another way to continue your education is to refine and specialize your skills. Getting certified in Google AdWords, or in search engine optimization (SEO), maybe hypertext markup language (HTML) or cascading style sheets (CSS), are each ways that you can show expertise in your specific area. This provides value to you, your employer, and your job. Finally, keeping yourself up to date on industry news is essential for success, as so many industry insiders noted. Read trade publications, join LinkedIn groups, and check out academic journals in your field to help grow your base of knowledge.

MENTORING

Throughout your college career, you may have heard the benefits of finding a mentor. You may even have a mentor in a previous supervisor or college professor. Mentors are people who are senior to you in experience. They help you accurately assess your skills (Culberson, 2015), encourage you to pursue new opportunities, and provide unwavering support throughout your career. But mentors do not just show up in your life when you need them. You need to seek out a mentor and should not be afraid to ask someone to be your mentor—within reason (Myers, 2016). Mentoring relationships should emerge naturally and not be forced. As Sheryl Sandberg (2013) notes, you should not ask someone to be your mentor just because you want him or her as your mentor. Instead, your mentor should be someone who makes sense in your industry and career trajectory. It should be a person you already know and feel comfortable interacting with for maximized potential. As so many of the industry insiders mentioned throughout this book, mentors have helped them succeed in their careers and have provided invaluable guidance. In addition to finding a mentor, you should try to be a mentor whenever possible. Consider remaining involved with your school after you graduate and helping to mentor rising juniors and seniors by leveraging your own unique experience. The best mentorships are two-way mutually beneficial relationships, and there is no reason that you cannot share your experience to help someone else on their professional journey.

In conclusion, starting a new job is stressful, but learning how to fit in will help lower your stress and increase your potential for success. Learning through observation, being social, and continuing your learning beyond your collegiate career are key ways to find career success and independence. Finally, finding a mentor, as well as being a mentor, can enrich your professional experience.

REFERENCES

Adcock, D., Halborg, A., & Ross, C. (2001). *Marketing: Principles and practice* (4th ed.). Englewood Cliffs, NJ: Prentice Hall.

Advertising Educational Foundation. (2016). Career guide. Retrieved from http://www.aef.com/building-talent/career-guide

Allen, T. (1977). *Managing the flow of technology.* Cambridge, MA: MIT Press.

Altman, I., & Taylor, D. (1973). *Social penetration: The development of interpersonal relationships.* New York, NY: Holt, Reinhart & Winston.

American Marketing Association. (n.d.). About AMA: Definition of marketing. Retrieved from https://www.ama.org/AboutAMA/Pages/Definition-of-Marketing.aspx

American Press Institute. (2016). *What is journalism?* Retrieved from https://www.americanpressinstitute.org/journalism-essentials/what-is-journalism

American Society for Public Administration. (2016). ASPA history. Retrieved from http://www.aspanet.org/ASPA/About-ASPA/ASPA-History/ASPA/About-ASPA/ASPA-History/ASPA-History.aspx? hkey=04cb7033-c678-4d97-a826-f55a2676fd2d

Barrick, M., & Mount, M. (1991). The Big Five personality dimensions and job performance: A meta-analysis. *Personnel Psychology, 44*, 1–26.

Berger, A. (1995). *Essentials of mass communication theory.* Thousand Oaks, CA: Sage.

Blau, G. (1993). Further exploring the relationship between job search and voluntary individual turnover. *Personnel Psychology, 46*, 313–330.

Bradley, D. (2016). The four functions of mass communications. *Small Business.* Retrieved from http://smallbusiness.chron.com/four-functions-mass-communications-56326.html

Branch, J. (2012). Snow fall: The avalanche at Tunnel Creek. *The New York Times.* Retrieved from http://www.nytimes.com/projects/2012/snow-fall/#/?part=tunnel-creek

Brehm, S. (1985). *Intimate relationships.* New York, NY: McGraw-Hill.

Bretz, R., Boudreau, J., & Judge, T. (1994). Job search behavior of employed managers. *Personnel Psychology, 47*, 275–301.

Bridge, K., & Baxter, L. (1992). Blended relationships: Friends as work associates. *Western Journal of Communication, 56*, 200–225.

Brown, D., Cober, R., Kane, K., Levy, P., & Shalhoop, J. (2006). Proactive personality and the successful job search: A field study with college graduates. *Journal of Applied Psychology, 9*, 717–726.

Burks, A. (2016). *What is the job description for a brand ambassador?* Retrieved from http://work.chron.com/job-description-brand-ambassador-17805.html

CareerCast. (2017). Most stressful jobs of 2017. Retrieved from http://www.careercast.com/jobs-rated/most-stressful-jobs-2017

Careers in Music. (2015). Radio DJ. Retrieved from https://www.careersinmusic.com/radio-dj

Chuday, L. (2008). *NAB's guide to careers in radio* (2nd ed.). Retrieved from http://www.broadcastcareerlink.com/documents/NABRadioCareers.pdf

Clark, L., Karau, S., & Michalisin, M. (2012). Telecommuting attitudes and the Big Five personality dimensions. *Journal of Management Policy and Practice, 13*, 31–46.

Coco, M. (2000). Internships: A try before you buy arrangement. *SAM Advanced Management Journal, 65*, 41–47.

Commission on Public Relations Education. (2015). Industry-educator summit on public relations education: Summary report. Retrieved from http://www.commpred.org/_uploads/industry-educator-summit-summary-report.pdf

Costa, P., & McCrae, R. (1992). Normal personality assessment in clinical practice: The NEO personality inventory. *Psychological Assessment, 4*, 5–13.

Cozby, P. C. (1973). Self-disclosure: A literature review. *Psychological Bulletin, 79*, 73–91. doi:10.1037/h0033950

Culberson, R. (2015). The value of mentoring. *HuffPost*. Retrieved from http://www.huffingtonpost.com/ron-culberson-msw-csp/the-value-of-mentoring_b_6857454.html

DeFleur, M., & Dennis, E. (1993). *Understanding mass communication.* Boston, MA: Houghton Mifflin.

Deleon, M. (2015). The importance of emotional intelligence at work. *Entrepreneur.* Retrieved from https://www.entrepreneur.com/article/245755

Denhardt, J., & Denhardt, R. (2015). The new public service revisited. *Public Administration Review, 78*, 664–672.

Derlega, V. J., Metts, S., Petronio, S., & Margulis, S. T. (1993). *Self-disclosure*. Newbury Park, CA: Sage.

Dibner, B. (1959). *The Atlantic cable.* Norwalk, CT: Burndy Library.

Di Gregorio, V. (2012). Life as a publishing sales rep. Retrieved from http://www.publishingcrawl.com/2012/03/29/life-as-a-publishing-sales-rep

Doyle, A. (2014). How to use job search networking to find a job. Retrieved from http://jobsearch.about.com/cs/networking/a/networking.htm

Dubinsky, A., Howell, R., Ingram, T., & Bellenger, D. (1986). Salesforce socialization. *Journal of Marketing, 50*, 192–207.

Duenas, J. (2010). Marketing and advertising—Similarities and differences. Retrieved from http://ezinearticles.com/?Marketing-and-Advertising---Similarities-and-Differences&id=5415716

Eisenberg, E., & Goodall, H. (1997). *Organizational communication: Balancing creativity and constraint* (2nd ed.). New York, NY: St. Martin's Press.

Ethics in Marketing. (2016). What is marketing? Retrieved from http://www.knowthis.com/what-is-marketing/ethics-in-marketing

Ewen, S. (2001). *Captains of consciousness: Advertising and the social roots of the consumer culture* (Anniversary ed.). New York, NY: McGraw-Hill.

Fine, G. (1986). Friendships in the work place. In V. J. Derelega & B. A. Winstead (Eds.), *Friendship and social interaction* (pp. 185–206). New York, NY: Springer-Verlag.

Gerbner, G. (1998). Cultivation analysis: An overview. *Mass Communication & Society, 1*, 175–194.

Giving USA Foundation. (2016). See the numbers: Giving USA 2016 infographic. Retrieved from https://givingusa.org/see-the-numbers-giving-usa-2016-infographic

Glassdoor. (2016). Entry level advertising salaries. Retrieved from https://www.glassdoor.com/Salaries/entry-level-advertising-salary-SRCH_KO0,23.htm

Goldberg, L. (1990). An alternative "description of personality:" The Big Five factor structure. *Journal of Personality and Social Psychology, 59*, 1216–1229.

Goleman, D. (2005). *Emotional intelligence: Why it can matter more than IQ*. New York, NY: Bantam Books.

Gordon, J. (2010). 50 job search statistics you need to know. Retrieved from http://careerchangechallenge.com/50-job-search-statistics-you-need-to-know

Gottfried, J., & Shearer, E. (2016). News use across social media platforms 2016. Retrieved from http://www.journalism.org/2016/05/26/news-use-across-social-media-platforms-2016

Granovetter, M. (1995). *Getting a job: A study of contacts and careers* (2nd ed.). Chicago, IL: University of Chicago Press.

Greene, K., Derlega, V. J., & Mathews, A. (2006). Self-disclosure in personal relationships. In A. Vangelisti & D. Perlman (Eds.), *Cambridge handbook of personal relationships* (pp. 409–427). New York, NY: Cambridge University Press.

Grobman, G. (2008). *The nonprofit handbook: Everything you need to know to start and run your nonprofit organization*. Harrisburg, PA: White Hat Communications.

Hall, P. (1994). Historical perspectives on nonprofit organizations. In R. D. Herman and Associates (Eds.), *The Jossey-Bass handbook of nonprofit leadership and management* (pp. 3–43). San Francisco, CA: Jossey-Bass.

Han, L. (2013). Soft skills list—28 skills to working smart. Retrieved from https://bemycareercoach.com/soft-skills/list-soft-skills.html

Han, L. (2015). Hard skills vs. soft skills—Difference and importance. Retrieved from https://www.linkedin.com/pulse/hard-skills-vs-soft-difference-importance-hajar-lion-lssbb-pmp

Herman, L. (n.d.). 5 ways Twitter can help you reach your career goals. Retrieved from https://www.themuse.com/advice/5-ways-twitter-can-help-you-reach-your-career-goals

Holmes, R. (2015). 5 trends that will change how companies use social media in 2016. *Fast Company.* Retrieved from https://www.fastcompany.com/3054347/the-future-of-work/5-trends-that-will-change-how-companies-use-social-media-in-2016

Holmstrom, A., Russell, J., & Clare, D. (2013). Esteem support messages received during the job search: A test of the CETESM. *Communication Monographs, 80*, 220–242.

Holzer, H. (1987). Job search by employed and unemployed. *Industrial and Labor Relations Review, 40*, 601–611.

HR Council. (2016). Getting the right people. Job profile: Program director. Retrieved from http://hrcouncil.ca/hr-toolkit/right-people-job-descriptions-program-director.cfm

Hyder, S. (2014). 7 things you can do to build an awesome personal brand. *Forbes.* Retrieved from http://www.forbes.com/sites/shamahyder/2014/08/18/7-things-you-can-do-to-build-an-awesome-personal-brand/#5e7fe5fc1274

Idealist. (2016). Introduction to development and fundraising. Retrieved from http://www.idealist.org/info/Nonprofits/Dev1

Inc. (2016). Nonprofit organizations and human resources management. Retrieved from http://www.inc.com/encyclopedia/nonprofit-organizations-and-human-resources-management.html

International Monetary Fund and International Labor Organization. (2010). The challenges of growth, employment, and social cohesion. Retrieved from http://www.osloconference2010.org/discussionpaper.pdf

International Telecommunications Union. (2012). Radio regulations. Retrieved from http://www.itu.int/dms_pub/itu-s/oth/02/02/S02020000244501PDFE.PDF

Jensen, P., & Westergard-Nielsen, N. (1987). A search model applied to the transition from education to work. *Review of Economic Studies, 54*, 461–472.

Jones, N. (2012). Three central benefits of volunteering as a college student. Retrieved from http://www.pointsoflight.org/blog/2012/10/25/three-central-benefits-volunteering-college-student.

Judge, T., Higgins, C., Thoresen, C., & Barrick, M. (1999). The big five personality traits, general mental ability, and career success across the lifespan. *Personnel Psychology, 52*, 621–652.

Judge, T., Ilies, R., Bono, J., & Gerhardt, M. (2002). Personality and leadership: A qualitative and quantitative review. *Journal of Applied Psychology, 87*, 765–780.

Kanfer, R., Wanberg, C., & Kantrowitz, T. (2001). A personality-motivational analysis and meta-analytic review. *Journal of Applied Psychology, 86*, 837–855.

Katz, E., & Lazarsfeld, P. (1955). *Personal influence.* New York, NY: The Free Press.

Kemp, S. (2016). Digital in 2016. *We Are Social.* Retrieved from http://www.slideshare.net/wearesocialsg/digital-in-2016

Kennedy, S. (n.d.). How new graduates can use part-time work to gain valuable job skills. Retrieved from https://www.monster.com/career-advice/article/job-skills-part-time-job

Kettl, D., & Fessler, D. (2009). *The politics of the administrative process.* Washington, DC: CQ Press.

Kotler, P. (1991). *Marketing management: Analysis, planning, and control* (8th ed.). Englewood Cliffs, NJ: Prentice Hall.

Kovach, B., & Rosenstiel, T. (2007). *The elements of journalism: What newspeople should know and the public should expect.* New York, NY: Three Rivers Press.

Kram, K., & Isabella, L. (1985). Mentoring alternatives: The role of peer relationships in career development. *Academy of Management Journal, 28*, 110–132.

Lasswell, H. (1942). The politically significant content of the press: Coding procedures. *Journalism Quarterly, 19,* 12-23.

Lasswell, H. (1948). The structure and function of communication and society: The communication of ideas. *Institute for Religious and Social Studies*, 203–243.

Lebel, J. (n.d.). Internships: A win-win for employers and students. Retrieved from https://www.experience.com/alumnus/article?channel_id=internships&source_page=home&article_id=article_1208895873387

Life, B. (2013). Why gaining work experience is more important than your education. *HuffPost.* Retrieved from http://www.huffingtonpost.com/brazen-life/why-gaining-work-experien_b_3750261.html

Lindlof, T., & Taylor, B. (2011). *Qualitative communication research methods.* Thousand Oaks, CA: Sage.

LinkedIn. (2016). About us. Retrieved from https://press.linkedin.com/about-linkedin

Loretto, P. (2016). Why students should consider doing one or more internships. Retrieved from https://www.thebalance.com/why-students-should-consider-internships-1986815

Losowsky, A. (2013). Indie bookstores file lawsuit against Amazon. *HuffPost.* Retrieved from http://www.huffingtonpost.com/2013/02/20/drm-lawsuit-independent-bookstores-amazon_n_2727519.html

Lu, K., & Holcomb, J. (2016). Digital news audience: Fact sheet. Pew Research Center. Retrieved from http://www.journalism.org/2016/06/15/digital-news-audience-fact-sheet

Magazines.com. (2016). The history of magazines. Retrieved from https://www.magazines.com/history-of-magazines

Martin, C. (n.d.). Nonverbal communications: Escape the pitfalls. Retrieved from https://www.monster.com/career-advice/article/nonverbal-communications-interview

Matsa, K., & Mitchell, A. (2013). News magazines: By the numbers. *State of the News Media, 2013.* Retrieved from http://www.stateofthemedia.org/2013/news-magazines-embracing-their-digital-future/news-magazines-by-the-numbers

Mau, W., & Kopischke, A. (2001). Job search methods, job search outcomes, and job satisfaction of recent college graduates: A comparison of race and sex. *Journal of Employment Counseling, 38*, 141–149.

McCombs, M., & Shaw, D. (1972). The agenda-setting function of mass media. *Public Opinion Quarterly, 36*, 176–187.

Milliot, J. (2010). Self-published titles topped 764,000 in 2009 as traditional output dipped. *Publishers Weekly.* Retrieved from http://www.publishersweekly.com/pw/by-topic/industry-news/publishing-and-marketing/article/42826-self-published-titles-topped-764-000-in-2009-as-traditional-output-dipped.html

Monster. (2016). Marketing jobs. Retrieved from http://www.monster.com/career-advice/article/marketing-jobs

Mount, M., Barrick, M., & Stewart, G. (1998). Five factor model of personality and performance in jobs involving interpersonal interactions. *Human Performance, 11*, 145–166.

Myers, C. (2016). Mentorship is key to career success for young professionals. *Forbes.* Retrieved from http://www.forbes.com/sites/chrismyers/2016/02/21/mentorship-is-key-to-career-success-for-young-professionals/#7084eb1f7091

Needle, D. (2004). *Business in context: An introduction to business and its environment.* Boston, MA: Cengage Learning.

Newbold, C. (2016). Design trends in 2015: Keep yourself current! Retrieved from http://thevisualcommunicationguy.com/2016/04/29/design-trends-in-2015-keep-yourself-current

O'Connor, B. (2014). How to get a job in book publishing. *Bustle.* Retrieved from https://www.bustle.com/articles/33160-how-to-get-a-job-in-book-publishing

Odden, C., & Sias, P. (1997). World views as context for communication studies. In J. L. Owen (Ed.), *Context and communication behavior* (pp. 17–40). Reno, NV: Context Press.

O'Keefe, A., & Pollay, R. (1996). Deadly targeting of women in promoting cigarettes. *Journal of the American Medical Women's Association, 51*, 67–69.

Orcutt, W. (1930). *The magic of the book.* Boston, MA: Little, Brown.

Orlik, P. (1992). *The electronic media.* Needham Heights, MA: Allyn & Bacon.

O'Sullivan, A., & Sheffrin, S. (2003). *Economics: Principles in action*. Upper Saddle River, NJ: Prentice Hall.

Parks, S. (2009). History of nonprofits in America. Retrieved from https://shannon laliberteparks.wordpress.com/2009/09/21/history-of-non-profits-in-america

PayScale. (2017). Recruiter salary. Retrieved from http://www.payscale.com/research/US/Job=Recruiter/Salary

Perry, J., & Christensen, R. (2015). *Handbook of public administration.* San Francisco, CA: Wiley.

Peterson, T. (n.d.). Interview tips to help you land a job. Retrieved from https://www.monster.com/career-advice/article/job-interview-pointers-fogarty

Pratt, J. (1984). Home telecommuting: A study of its pioneers. *Technological Forecasting and Social Change, 25,* 1–14.

Price, R., & Vinokur, A. (1995). Supporting career transitions in a time of organizational downsizing. In M. London (Ed.), *Employees, careers, and job creation* (pp. 191–209). San Francisco, CA: Jossey-Bass.

Public Relations Society of America. (2012). Public relations defined: A modern definition for the new era of public relations. Retrieved from www.prsa.org

Publishing. (2017, November 23). In *Merriam-Webster.* Retrieved from https://www.merriam-webster.com/dictionary/publishing

Publishing Trends. (2011). The skills publishers need: A self-evaluation. Retrieved from http://www.publishingtrends.com/2011/02/the-skills-publishers-need-a-self-evaluation

Rawlins, W. (1992). *Friendship matters: Communication, dialectics, and the life course.* New York, NY: Aldine de Gruyter.

Reuters. (2008). Reuters, from pigeons to multimedia merger. Retrieved from http://www.reuters.com/article/us-reuters-thomson-chronology-idUSL1849100620080219

Ricardo, A. (2015). Why internships are important for students and employers. Retrieved from https://www.linkedin.com/pulse/why-internships-important-students-employers-andy-ricardo

Ruggiero, T. (2000). Uses and gratifications theory in the 21st century. *Mass Communication & Society, 3,* 3–37.

Saks, A., & Ashforth, B. (1999). Effects of individual differences and job search behaviors on the employment status of recent university graduates. *Journal of Vocational Behavior, 54,* 335–349.

Sandberg, S. (2013). *Lean in: Women, work and the will to lead.* New York, NY: Knopf.

Schwabel, D. (2009). Personal branding 101: How to discover and create your brand. Retrieved from http://mashable.com/2009/02/05/personal-branding-101/#0wT3tWKrsEqB

Search Engine Land. (2016). What is search marketing? Retrieved from http://searchengineland.com/guide/what-is-sem

Shepard, A. (2011). NPR's Gifford's mistake: Re-learning the lesson of checking sources. Retrieved from http://www.npr.org/sections/ombudsman/2011/01/11/132812196/nprs-giffords-mistake-re-learning-the-lesson-of-checking-sources

Shin, L. (2014). How to use LinkedIn: 5 smart steps to career success. *Forbes*. Retrieved from http://www.forbes.com/sites/laurashin/2014/06/26/how-to-use-LinkedIn-5-smart-steps-to-career-success/2/#29989e2d3bab

Sias, P., & Cahill, D. (1998). From coworkers to friends: The development of peer friendships in the workplace. *Western Journal of Communication, 62*, 273–299.

Smith, J. (2013). How to ace the 50 most common interview questions. *Forbes*. Retrieved from http://www.forbes.com/sites/jacquelynsmith/2013/01/11/how-to-ace-the-50-most-common-interview-questions/#f5504e448737

Smith, K. (2016). 44 Twitter statistics for 2016. Retrieved from https://www.brandwatch.com/blog/44-twitter-stats-2016

Smith, S. A., & Brunner, S. R. (2017). To reveal or conceal: Using communication privacy management theory to understand disclosures in the workplace. *Management Communication Quarterly, 31*, 429–446. doi:10.1177/0893318917692896

Smith, S. A., Patmos, A., & Pitts, M. (2015). Communication and teleworking: A study of communication channel satisfaction, personality, and job satisfaction for teleworking employees. *International Journal of Business Communication*. doi:10.1177/2329488415589101

Stanton, W. (1984). *Fundamentals of marketing*. New York, NY: McGraw-Hill.

Statista. (2016). Statistics and facts about the advertising industry in the United States. Retrieved from https://www.statista.com/topics/979/advertising-in-the-us

Surbhi, S. (2015). Difference between marketing and advertising. Retrieved from http://keydifferences.com/difference-between-marketing-and-advertising.html

Suttle, R. (n.d.). Does a spokesperson get paid? *Chron.com*. Retrieved from http://work.chron.com/spokesperson-paid-21919.html

Tucker, D., Unwin, G., & Unwin, P. (2015). History of publishing. *Encyclopedia Brittanica*. Retrieved from https://www.britannica.com/topic/publishing

Undercover Recruiter. (n.d.). Retrieved from https://theundercoverrecruiter.com/6-interview-types-you-must-know-candidate

U.S. Bureau of Labor Statistics. (2014). Employment situation summary. Retrieved from http://www.bls.gov/news.release/empsit.nr0.htm

U.S. Bureau of Labor Statistics. (2017a, October 24). Advertising, promotions, and marketing managers. Occupational outlook handbook. Retrieved from https://www.bls.gov/ooh/management/advertising-promotions-and-marketing-managers.htm

U.S. Bureau of Labor Statistics. (2017b, October 24). Public relations specialists. Occupational outlook handbook. Retrieved from https://www.bls.gov/ooh/media-and-communication/public-relations-specialists.htm

U.S. Bureau of Labor Statistics. (2017c, October 24). Reporters, correspondents, and broadcast news analysts. Occupational outlook handbook. Retrieved from https://www.bls.gov/ooh/media-and-communication/reporters-correspondents-and-broadcast-news-analysts.htm

U.S. Census Bureau. (2017). U.S. population. Retrieved from https://www.census.gov/topics/population.html

U.S. Department of Labor. (2015). Occupational outlook handbook. Retrieved from http://www.bls.gov/ooh/home.htm

U.S. Department of Labor. (2016). Publishing industries (except Internet). Retrieved from http://www.bls.gov/iag/tgs/iag511.htm

USC Annenberg. (2007). PR management database. Retrieved from www.annenberg.usc.edu/sprc

Vivian, J. (2011). *The media of mass communication* (10th ed.). Boston, MA: Allyn & Bacon.

Vogt, P. (n.d.). Six key interview answers employers need to hear. Retrieved from https://www.monster.com/career-advice/article/six-answers-interviewers-need

Wanberg, C., Hough, L., & Song, Z. (2002). Predictive validity of a multidisciplinary model of reemployment success. *Journal of Applied Psychology, 87,* 1100–1120.

Wanberg, C., Kanfer, R., & Banas, J. (2000). Predictors and outcomes of networking intensity among unemployed job seekers. *Journal of Applied Psychology, 85,* 491–503.

Wetfeet. (2012). Career overview: Broadcasting. Retrieved from https://www.wetfeet.com/articles/career-overview-broadcasting

Wigmore, I. (2013). Definition: Public sector. Retrieved from http://whatis.techtarget.com/definition/private-sector

Wilcox, D., Cameron, G., & Reber, B. (2015). *Public relations: Strategies and tactics* (11th ed.). Upper Saddle River, NJ: Pearson.

Wilcox, D., Cameron, G., Reber, B., & Shin, J. (2013). *Think public relations*. Boston, MA: Pearson.

Wilson, W. (1887). The study of administration. *Political Science Quarterly, 2,* 197–222.

INDEX

ABOUT THE AUTHOR

Stephanie A. Smith, PhD, is an assistant professor of communication at Virginia Tech. She leverages her professional experience in marketing and public relations (PR) within her teaching and research endeavors. Specifically, she studies professional development and job searching strategies for entry-level employees and recent college graduates. She is passionate about bridging the gap between education and practice and helping prepare college students for successful professional careers.